TOL, NEW̱ SEN TŦE SOȽ
|
I KNOW THE ROAD

ARP Books (Arbeiter Ring Publishing)
205-70 Arthur Street
Winnipeg, Manitoba
Treaty 1 Territory and Historic Métis Nation Homeland Canada R3B 1G7
arpbooks.org

Cover design by Bret Parenteau.
Interior layout by Relish New Brand Experience.
Printed and bound in Canada by Imprimerie Gauvin on certified FSC ® paper.

Canada Council for the Arts Conseil des arts du Canada
MANITOBA ARTS COUNCIL CONSEIL DES ARTS DU MANITOBA
Canada
Manitoba

ARP Books acknowledges the generous support of the Manitoba Arts Council and the Canada Council for the Arts for our publishing program. We acknowledge the financial support of the Government of Canada and the Province of Manitoba through the Book Publishing Tax Credit and the Book Publisher Marketing Assistance Program of Manitoba Culture, Heritage, and Tourism.

Library and Archives Canada Cataloguing in Publication

Title: TOL, NEW̱ SEN TŦE SOȽ : I know the road : challenging white supremacy and anti-Indigenous racism in academia / Jack Horne.
Other titles: I know the road
Names: Horne, Jack, author.
Identifiers: Canadiana (print) 20240375203 | Canadiana (ebook) 20240375319 | ISBN 9781927886847 (softcover) | ISBN 9781927886854 (ebook)
Subjects: LCSH: Critical pedagogy. | LCSH: Racism in higher education. | LCSH: Discrimination in higher education. | CSH: W̱SÁNEĆ.
Classification: LCC LC196 .H67 2024 | DDC 370.11/5—dc23

TOL, NEW̱ SEN ȾŦE SȮȽ

|

I KNOW THE ROAD

Challenging White Supremacy and Anti-Indigenous Racism in Academia

Jack Horne

ARP Books | Winnipeg

CONTENTS

Prologue 11

X̱I,ȺM
(Storytime)

NEȾE
(One)

Stoles 17
Introduction 21
Research 23
Early W̱sáneć Resarch 27
Sx̱i¸Ám (Storytime) 41
Connecting The Dots 43

X̱I,ȺM
(Storytime)

ĆESE
(Two)

Eric M. 49
Researcher Positionality 53
Researcher Education Journey 56
Post Secondary Education—The Return 61
Camosun College Years: 2008–2010 61
The University Of Victoria: 2010–2013 64
York University: 2013–2014 70
Trent University: 2014–2023 77

SX̱I¸ÁM

(Storytime)

LI̱W̱

(Three)

Lelilen̲ 99

A W̱sáneć Paradigm 101

W̱sáneć Knowledge and Colonization 103

Tol, Neẉ Sen Tte Sol 106

Ignorance and the University Experience 107

Centering Indigenous Knowledges 112

An Indigenous and/or W̱sáneć Paradigm 127

Embodied W̱sáneć Knowledge 147

Embodied Indigenous Knowledge 149

W̱sáneć Ways of Being (Ontology) 152

W̱sáneć Ways of Knowing (Epistemology) 155

W̱sáneć Ways of Doing (Axiology and Methodology) 157

Relational, Interrelated, and Relational Accountability of W̱sáneć Living 160

Contemporary Embodied W̱sáneć Knowledge Transfer 167

S<u>X</u>I¸ÁM

(Storytime)

Ṉ<u>N</u>OS

(Four)

S¢i¸No<u>n</u>et 173
I, A W̱sáneć Artist and Academic 174
W̱sáneć Places and Spaces 174
Muriel Miguel and Storyweaving Performance Methodology 177
The Picnic *as Embodied W̱sáneć Knowledge Transfer* 184
W̱sáneć First, W̱sáneć Artist Second, and Academic Third 188

SX̱I¸ÁM

(Storytime)

L̄ḴÁĆES

(Five)

¢ł Ćelál I Esebt Es 191
Sx̱i¸Ám (*One Final Storytime*) 191
The Picnic 193
REFERENCES 201

There was this picture, and it reminded me of a story...

—Jack Horne,
The Picnic

Within Indigenous writing, a prologue structures space for introductions while serving a bridging function for non-Indigenous readers. It is a precursory signal to the careful reader that woven throughout the varied forms of our writing—analytical, reflective, expository—there will be story, for our story is who we are.

—Margaret Kovach,
Indigenous Methodologies: Characteristics, Conversations, and Contexts

The truth about stories is, that's all we are.

—Thomas King,
The Truth About Stories: A Native Narrative

PROLOGUE

My name is Jack Horne. My traditional name is Chowithet. I am from the W̱SÁNEĆ Nation, located at the southern tip of Vancouver Island. My mother's name is Elsie Smith, and she is from the W̱JOȽEȽP (Tsartlip) reserve located within the W̱SÁNEĆ Nation. My dad's name is George Horne, and he is from the SȾÁUTW̱ (Tsawout) reserve located within the W̱SÁNEĆ Nation. It is important for me to self-identify through my parents' traditional village areas so that anyone from our territory will know who my family is. This is done so that they may better understand what my lineage is and ascertain if we are related. The purpose of this prologue is for me to self-locate and to position myself as a W̱SÁNEĆ researcher "at the centre of the project and all that this entails."[1]

My life has moved in cycles. I was born at the Resthaven Hospital, located at the heart of traditional W̱SÁNEĆ territories. I spent the first three years of my life living in the W̱JOȽEȽP reserve, after which we moved to the SȾÁUTW̱ reserve. I lived there until I left the W̱SÁNEĆ territories shortly after graduating from high school. During the first nineteen years of my life, I was introduced to and participated in many traditional W̱SÁNEĆ activities, including our sacred and ancient longhouse practices. I spent a great deal

1 Graham Smith, in Margaret Kovach, *Indigenous Methodologies: Characteristics, Conversations, and Contexts* (Toronto: University of Toronto Press, 2009), 90.

of time either fishing with my dad in traditional W̱SÁNEĆ waters (frontispiece) or travelling on special occasions to picnic on one of the surrounding islands, which has been used by my ancestors since time immemorial (frontispiece).

I began taking dance classes in high school at the age of seventeen, and by eighteen I had my first professional theatre job. This would prove to be the beginning of a career that would continue for the next twenty-five years. When I had retired from theatre, I began Indigenous Studies at Camosun College. I retired in large part because I was getting older, but also because I had legitimate concerns about my ageing mom's health. I moved in with her and my younger sister and began to help with her care, as is common in many Indigenous families. I was able to spend her final two years with her, just sitting and talking in what was to become a very important personal oral tradition and knowledge transfer. During this time, I had the opportunity to ask her questions about issues I was studying, such as Indian agents or residential schools. More importantly, I was able to ask her questions about our longhouse practices and about W̱SÁNEĆ ways of being. I had the opportunity to ask why certain things were done in a particular way, or to ask what the meaning was behind a specific action or event. In this way, traditional W̱SÁNEĆ Knowledge was shared with me through time-honoured oral transmission.

When my mom passed away suddenly, I dropped out of school and went through my own grieving process. When I returned to W̱SÁNEĆ territories, I volunteered for and was initiated into our longhouse practices. These practices are distinct and very private, so I need to be very clear: I will not be revealing any sacred knowledge or providing any type of insider look at the inner workings of W̱SÁNEĆ longhouses in my work here. I am more interested in how our practices are embodied, transmitted, and used to help us as W̱SÁNEĆ people to heal and survive. When I returned to post-secondary education it was with a renewed fire. I studied at the

University of Victoria and completed my undergraduate degree in political science. During this time, I also wrote a play in honour of my mom, titled *Indigenous Like Me*, which premiered in November 2012. In this play, I integrated my experience as a theatre professional with my education in Indigenous Studies and political science, and incorporated traditional W̱SÁNEĆ Knowledges in a theatre format. I wrote this play as a personal healing mechanism, and its importance did not become apparent to me until much later.

Stories. Personal stories. Family stories. W̱SÁNEĆ oral narratives as stories. There is something poetic about the cycles that keep returning me to W̱SÁNEĆ traditions and connections to my territories. When I think of my teachings, I think of my mom because she is the one who gave them to me. When I wrote *Indigenous Like Me*, it was for her. The final scene of the play reads:

> *Now, no matter what I do I hear her voice. Doesn't matter if I am studying the Indian Act at University or the history of colonialism, residential schools, or even feminism because it's her voice I hear. It's her teachings I remember and her life I think of when I approach those issues. And it makes me happy.*
>
> *It makes me happy because I realize that makes me Indigenous Like Her.*

After my mom passed away, my sisters found an un-mailed letter she wrote to me. At the time, I quickly read it and put it away. I recently found that letter again and I was so grateful to see her words in her own handwriting:

> *Sorry Son.*
>
> *Things are not so good at home, so far we have lost three of our Elders here, sure makes me feel bad. Uncle Henry Smith was one, he was one of our last grandfathers, we don't have any more. Love Mom*

My Mom knew the importance of W̱SÁNEĆ Elder knowledge, and in 1994 she was aware of the loss. Words from the past cycled around to my present informing me of the direction my research should take. I had but to listen and heed her words to acknowledge how my life is made up of cycles returning me to all things W̱SÁNEĆ.

HÍSW̱ḴE SIAM

X̲ I,ÁM

(STORYTIME)

NET/E

(ONE)

STOLES[1]

A long time ago on an island near the SȾÁUTW̱[2] village a small family was gathering food to store for the winter. ȽELTOS[3] hid the tragedy about to unfold on SḰŦÁMEN[4] in an area which eventually became know as ȾELXOLEU[5]—"The Place of Defeat." ȾELXOLEU is where this story begins.

SWÍḴE[6] stopped gathering seafood for a moment to take a breath and view the beauty of the day. He closed his eyes and felt the late summer sunshine on his face, along with the steady breeze from the sea. He listened to the exuberant chatter of his two children, no doubt a steady barrage of endless questions directed at their SILE,[7] and heard her ever-patient responses. He opened his eyes to look toward where his STOLES gathered ȽÁUḴEM.[8] SWÍḴE momentarily furrowed his brow in remembrance of her fitful night, which had been interrupted by prescient dreams. He waved an arm

1 Wife
2 Tsawout
3 Currently named James Island
4 Currently named Sidney Island
5 The Place of Defeat
6 Man
7 Grandmother
8 Mussel

to wake her from her daydream and both laughed as he mimed for her to resume her task. Their shared eye contact sent a jolt of love that threatened to burst both hearts as they returned to gathering food for winter storage.

STOLES briefly scanned the beach until she spotted her two daughters and her mother-in-law gathering clams. The children listened intently to the directions of their elder while eagerly digging up clams, between splashing each other with saltwater from the warm tidal pools dotted along on the beach. The new baby kicked, and STOLES placed a hand over her abdomen and thought, "This one will be a good runner," before scooping up her ŚȾEȽḰIṈEȽ[9] and returning to work.

The ŚȾEȽḰIṈEȽ had originally come from the femur of a large elk. The animal had fallen hard during a hunt and had fractured its powerful leg bone. As a result, it was decided to create a series of bone implements with it. The smaller fragments were further splintered, and the pieces used for sewing needles and fishing hooks. The slightly larger sections were carefully split using a stone WIYĆ[10] and then carefully worked against a rock until they were ready to be carved into jewelry or objects to be included in carvings. The strongest pieces were distributed among the families and similarly worked until the strong bones had their sharp edges dulled. The ŚȾEȽḰIṈEȽs eventually became a subconscious extension of the wielders' arms. Over time, the implements became personal and valued treasures, in large part because the owners' hands and the ŚȾEȽḰIṈEȽs grew into each other's forms.

STOLES had been troubled all morning by the strange dreams from the night before, and the images would not reveal themselves to her. Nor would they let her enjoy this beautiful day. She sighed and absentmindedly reached down into the water below as she watched her daughters squeal in delight when one of the clams sent up a spray from its hiding spot. STOLES's practiced fingers located the

9 Awl
10 Wedge

largest specimen, and without looking, she wedged her ŚŦEŁḰIṈEŁ between it and the hard stone. Countless hours of practice meant that STOLES had developed impressive strength in her hands, forearms, and wrists. The ŁÁUḴEM easily gave way, and STOLES didn't even examine the specimen before dropping it into the cedar basket by her side.

The kicking of her ḴAḴ[11] and the spray from the clam made her sigh in resignation, giving in to her full bladder. She picked up her basket of ŁÁUḴEM so that a clever animal wouldn't make a lunch of all her hard work. Just as STOLES reached the edge of the forest, terrified sounds erupted and made her heart stop.

11 Baby

INTRODUCTION

Academia remains an unwelcoming space for Indigenous scholars, and the space it does cede to Indigenous Knowledge is dictated and narrowly defined. Academia remains jealous, competitive, and territorial when it comes to negotiating space for alternative knowledges. In response to the question of how I, a W̱SÁNEĆ artist and academic, use embodied W̱SÁNEĆ Knowledge in my artistic and academic work, this writing advocates for a move away from standard social sciences theories, methodologies, and paradigms while forcefully insisting on an Indigenous—and more specifically, a W̱SÁNEĆ—paradigm. Accomplishing this requires a negotiation of embodied W̱SÁNEĆ Knowledge, performance studies theory, and western eurocentric social sciences paradigms. This combination is ambiguous at best, existing in an uneasy tripartite division. The challenge for me as a W̱SÁNEĆ researcher has been maintaining a focus on embodied W̱SÁNEĆ Knowledge while negotiating the perils of graduate studies. An intentional benefit of this research is the establishment of an Indigenous and/or W̱SÁNEĆ paradigm in opposition to the social sciences rhetoric I came into conflict with during my tumultuous PhD university experience. How I arrived at this fortuitous place and the journey that very nearly broke me are articulated in the following chapters.

The previous story (STOLES) is an introduction to W̱SÁNEĆ Knowledge in the standard written format. It is intended to illustrate how Indigenous storytelling can disseminate multiple aspects of Indigenous Knowledges. In this case the story articulates W̱SÁNEĆ history, W̱SÁNEĆ language, W̱SÁNEĆ connection to specific territorial spaces, and W̱SÁNEĆ resource gathering practices. The purpose and intent of this book is to move beyond the written English language to contemporize traditional W̱SÁNEĆ ways of teaching and learning. W̱SÁNEĆ teaching and knowledge were never written, but instead performed through stories, songs, dances, practices on the land and sea, or through ceremonies. They prioritized experiential learning through watching and doing. It is for this reason that I chose to focus on the performativity of traditional W̱SÁNEĆ Knowledges and explore the ways that I can contemporize those knowledges through theatre and performance, and the study of those practices.

STOLES, as it is currently written, is an example of how W̱SÁNEĆ Knowledge is expressed from the colonizer perspective. It is flat and intended to be consumed through reading alone, likely as a solitary endeavour with no outside input required. But imagine for a moment if this piece of writing were taken off the flat page and brought to life through sound and movement. The story could be performed as a monologue for a classroom of students, or at an academic conference, a performance festival, or any other location. Ideally, this story would be taken and explored by the previously mentioned groups using experiential learning. The result would be a style of teaching and learning traditional W̱SÁNEĆ Knowledges that used more than just the mind. That, in turn, would be more in line with traditional W̱SÁNEĆ Knowledge transfer. This would change the entire story dynamic—bringing it to life by including sound and movement as an alternative to the usual learning through reading. Instead of existing only on the flat page, the story would then have the capacity to impart W̱SÁNEĆ Knowledge through embodied experiential learning. The learning outcomes for the workshop participants or audience members would be multifold. Participants or audience members would end up learning some of the SENĆOŦEN language, W̱SÁNEĆ history, W̱SÁNEĆ place names, and W̱SÁNEĆ resource gathering practices in an engaged and entertaining way, achieving holistic learning through embodied W̱SÁNEĆ Knowledge transfer.

RESEARCH

Performance studies theory has been exploring the connections between culture, anthropology, performance, ritual, and theatre through the work of scholars such as Victor Turner and Richard Schechner.[12] Turner examined the components of rituals such as coming of age or death rituals in order to deconstruct the process and reveal the ways that rituals relate to theatrical performances. Both Turner and Schechner acknowledge the work of Erving Goffman as a precursor to performance studies. Goffman's foundational book *The Presentation of Self in Everyday Life* examines how each of us naturally play multiple roles in our daily lives.[13] Schechner elaborated on Goffman and Turner's theories, moving beyond ritual to encompass any activity, which included what he termed "twice-behaved" behaviour.[14] His work opened performance studies to the vast field of opportunity it is today. Diana Taylor is a South American professor of performance studies and Spanish at New York University and founding director of the Hemispheric Institute of Performance and Politics. In *The Archive and the Repertoire*, Taylor posits the rise in prominence and favouring of

12 Victor Turner, *From Ritual to Theatre: The Human Seriousness of Play* (New York: Performing Arts Journal Publications, 1982); Richard Schechner, *Performance Theory* (New York: Routledge, 1988; Richard Schechner, *The Future of Ritual: Writings on Culture and Performance* (New York: Routledge, 1993).

13 Erving Goffman, *The Presentation of Self in Everyday Life* (New York: Anchor Books, 1959).

14 Richard Schechner and Victor Turner, *Between Theater & Anthropology* (Philadelphia: University of Pennsylvania Press, 1985).

the written word in western society over *embodied* knowledge.[15] Taylor gives a brief explanation for the terms "archive" and the "repertoire" as "the *archive* of supposedly enduring materials (i.e., texts, documents, buildings, bones) and the so-called ephemeral *repertoire* of embodied practice/knowledge (i.e., spoken language, dance, sports, ritual)."[16] In other words, anything tangible or archivable in western society becomes more legitimate than the non-archivable. Consequently museums, libraries, and even computer data become important sources of western knowledge, while embodied Indigenous Knowledge remains a contested concept.

Embodied Indigenous Knowledges are those ephemeral practices Diana Taylor refers to as they relate to Indigenous Nations. The W̱SÁNEĆ Nation is largely a peninsula and traditional W̱SÁNEĆ territory includes that peninsula and the surrounding islands. Resource gathering practices on the land and the sea form a large part of those practices referred to by Diana Taylor as ephemeral—but which I understand as embodied W̱SÁNEĆ Knowledge. Embodied W̱SÁNEĆ Knowledge also includes our stories, our ceremonies, and our traditional dancing practiced in our longhouses. Each of these activities and more will be explored throughout this text and in conjunction with performance studies theories form the core of my work. The W̱SÁNEĆ Nation is one of many Indigenous nations that form a large contingent of Indigenous Peoples collectively referred to as the Coast Salish.

Coast Salish territories are located on the west coast of North America. They include a sizable portion of southeast Vancouver Island and cross the Salish Sea onto the mainland of British Columbia. These territories proceed south from both of these points, past the government-imposed Canada/US border, and include a significant portion of Washington State and the Puget Sound. My nation, the W̱SÁNEĆ Nation, resides at the southern tip of Vancouver Island

15 Diana Taylor, *The Archive and the Repertoire: Performing Cultural Memory in the Americas* (Durham: Duke University Press, 2003).

16 Taylor, *The Archive and the Repertoire*, 19.

on what is now called the Saanich Peninsula (Saanich is the phonetic spelling of our traditional W̱SÁNEĆ name). Our territory once included the entire peninsula, many of the surrounding gulf islands, and stretched across Brentwood Bay to include much of the lands around Goldstream Provincial Park. The Oregon Treaty of 1846 imposed the Canadian/US border and separated W̱SÁNEĆ relatives into Canadian and US sides without consultation with any Indigenous groups.[17] Despite these factors and assimilationist government policies, the W̱SÁNEĆ people have maintained a deep connection with cultural practices through embodied Indigenous Knowledge transfer in the forms of stories, songs, rituals, and ancient longhouse practices. Embodied Indigenous Knowledge is malleable and adaptable to parallel the adaptability of our peoples, and so the knowledge can be contemporary although it may have originated a millennium ago. Contemporary Indigenous artists in North and South America use embodied Indigenous Knowledges in varied ways. For example, Floyd Favel-Starr has been using "Cree Performance Theory" as a method to teach Indigenous theatre from a distinctly Cree perspective, while the iconic Spiderwoman Theatre's Miguel sisters (Muriel, Gloria, and Lisa) have developed the highly complex Storyweaving performance methodology, which reaches back and connects them with their Kuna/Rappahannock Indigenous roots.[18]

In part, I explore embodied Indigenous Knowledge and its application to contemporary Indigenous theatre by using my experience

17 Walter N. Sage, "The Oregon Treaty of 1846," *Canadian Historical Review* 27,1 (1946), 349; Penelope Edmonds, "Unpacking Settler Colonialism's Urban Strategies: Indigenous Peoples in Victoria, British Columbia, and the Transition to a Settler-Colonial City," *Urban History Review/Revue D'Histoire Urbaine* 38, 2 (2010): 4–20; Douglas C. Harris, *Landing Native Fisheries: Indian Reserves and Fishing Rights in British Columbia, 1849–1925*, (Vancouver: UBC Press, 2008); Douglas C. Harris, "A Court Between: Aboriginal and Treaty Rights in the British Columbia Court of Appeal," *BC Studies* 162 (2009): 137–164.

18 Rob Appleford, *Aboriginal Drama and Theatre* (Toronto: Playwrights Canada Press, 2005).

as one of four co-directors over two years of an Indigenous summer theatre intensive hosted at Trent University. The Centre for Indigenous Theatre (CIT) hosted these summer theatre intensives in 2015 and 2016, with Muriel Miguel as the resident director. A diverse group of Indigenous youth from all over Canada convened at Trent University with the express purpose of engaging with Spiderwoman Theatre's Indigenous performance methodology. The CIT program addressed all four areas of the medicine wheel (mental, emotional, spiritual, physical) as the Indigenous youth were exposed to their individual embodied Indigenous knowledges. During this five-week workshop, I witnessed how creating stories from personal narratives and/or stories from their respective Indigenous Nations empowered the youth in the most profound ways. Indigenous scholars have written about the importance of storytelling for Indigenous communities from diverse disciplinary perspectives.[19] Their scholarship highlights how the theatre/storytelling format allows for a freedom of expression beyond what can be found in a classroom setting, and offers an alternative to the hegemonic eurocentric western pedagogy that currently dominates contemporary education.

19 Jo-ann Archibald, *Indigenous Storywork: Educating the Heart, Mind, Body, and Spirit* (Vancouver: UBC Press, 2008); Jo-Ann Episkenew, *Taking Back Our Spirits: Indigenous Literature, Public Policy, and Healing* (Winnipeg: University of Manitoba Press, 2009); Richard Paul Knowles and Monique Mojica, eds., "Introduction," in *Staging Coyote's Dream: An Anthology of First Nations Drama in English* (Toronto: Playwrights Canada Press, 2003), iii-vii; Manulani Aluli Meyer, *Hawaiian Knowing: Old Ways for Feeing a New World* (Hawaii: Koa Books, 1998); Ngũgĩ wa Thiong'o, *Decolonizing the Mind: The Politics of Language in African Literature* (London; Nairobi; Portsmouth, NH: J. Currey, 1986); Leanne Betasamosake Simpson, *Dancing On Our Turtle's Back: Stories of Nishnaabeg Re-creation, Resurgence and a New Emergence* (Winnipeg: ARP Books, 2011); Jace Weaver, *That the People Might Live: Native American Literatures and Native American Community* (New York: Oxford University Press, 1997); Shawn Wilson, *Research is Ceremony: Indigenous Research Methods* (Blackpoint NS: Fernwood Publishing, 2008).

In attempting to answer my research question, I discovered personal, professional, and institutional obstacles in my path. Articulating an Indigenous/W̱SÁNEĆ paradigm has been the ultimate challenge for me, and those institutional obstacles and the opposition I experienced from those in charge is one well-known aspect of the graduate journey for many Indigenous students. However, that offers little consolation when it is you who is considering giving up the pursuit of a doctorate. I recently viewed an online talk given by Dr. Eve Tuck where she spoke of her academic friends who "know intimately my doubts and the millions of tiny wounds that we accumulate on our way to what looks like, on the outside, like success."[20] I have never needed to hear those words as much as when I was slogging through the first draft of my dissertation and about to enter my eighth year of PhD studies. I had been determined to finish my PhD in four years, but people and events beyond my control caused me to experience setbacks. Some of those setbacks are described in the following pages and represent the journey that led me to this book. I refused to allow institutional racism and academic gatekeepers to defeat me, but instead took my cue from STOLES, picked up the broken pieces of my academic dreams, and finished the journey, despite and to spite those who would rather I fail.

EARLY W̱SÁNEĆ RESARCH

In 2012, I published "W̱SÁNEĆ: Emerging Land or Emerging People" in *The Arbutus Review* while I was still an undergraduate student at the University of Victoria.[21] I used the substantial library collection at the University of Victoria and several recordings made by W̱SÁNEĆ Elders in its writing. Because of my relationality as

20 Mark Spooner, "Eve Tuck: Biting the Hand That Feeds You," YouTube, August 12, 2015.

21 Jack Horne, "W̱SÁNEĆ: Emerging Land or Emerging People," *The Arbutus Review* 3,2 (2012): 6-19. Additional portions of the article have been used for the writing of this section.

a W̱SÁNEĆ community member, I was given access to W̱SÁNEĆ Elder recordings by a Tsawout band office worker. I describe these in the article:

> In 2001, the Tsawout band conducted interviews about traditional burial grounds, food gathering and plants to oppose a BC Hydro project to install a natural gas pipeline in traditional W̱SÁNEĆ fishing territories. Excerpts from the Elder interviews contain important information on the traditional uses and areas of resource extraction for W̱SÁNEĆ Tsawout peoples.[22]

W̱SÁNEĆ territories once encompassed the entire Saanich Peninsula, many of the surrounding islands, and extended south into the mainland of Washington State. With the signing of the Oregon treaty in 1846, W̱SÁNEĆ territories and people were divided into Canadian or American sides.[23] As a result, family ties were disrupted, and families on each side of the border were left to face different government policies. The W̱SÁNEĆ Nation in Canada is currently divided into five separate reserves located in the areas known today as Tsawout, Tsartlip, Pauquachin, Tseycum, and Malahat. While a great deal of scholarship has been written about the Indigenous Peoples of British Columbia, there has been remarkably little written about the W̱SÁNEĆ Nation. There have been numerous books and journal articles published on the subject of colonial resettlement in British Columbia.[24] The study of Indigenous Peoples in British Columbia has been approached from the cultural relativist perspective found in the works of prolific writer and anthropologist Franz Boas, and British Columbian

22 Horne, "W̱SÁNEĆ: Emerging Land or Emerging People," 12.

23 Sage, "The Oregon Treaty of 1846."

24 See Wilson Duff, "The Fort Victoria Treaties," *Journal of BC studies* 3 (fall 1969): 3–57; Cole Harris, *The Resettlement of British Columbia: Essays on Colonialism and Geographical Change* (Vancouver: UBC Press,1997; Cole Harris, *Making Native Space: Colonialism, Resistance, and Reserves in British Columbia* (Vancouver: UBC Press, 2002).

Indigenous Nations have similarly been examined through ethnographic approaches found in the work of anthropologists such as Wilson Duff.[25] Finally, an overabundance of BC Treaty and Douglas or Fort Victoria Treaty books, chapters in books, and journal articles are available online and in print.[26] Describing Boas in *How Did Colonialism Dispossess?* Cole Harris writes, "Boas had little interest in the native societies around him (which, he thought, were becoming civilized), except insofar as they supplied informants about earlier, precontact times."[27] It is for this reason that cultural and personal biases need to be taken into account when engaging with the plethora of early non-Indigenous writings about the Indigenous Nations found in British Columbia.[28]

Thousands of years before James Douglas approached the W̱SÁNEĆ people and proposed his agreements, W̱SÁNEĆ people lived and travelled across what is now called the Saanich Peninsula. Oral tradition can be traced back millennia and includes our own creation and flood stories. A great example of the W̱SÁNEĆ flood story can be found in Wolff-Michael Roth and Angela Calabrese

25 See Franz Boas, *Tsimshian Texts* (Washington, DC: Government Printing Office, 1902); Franz Boas, *Folk-tales of Salishan and Sahaptin Tribes* (New York: G.E. Strechert & Co., 1917); Franz Boas, *Kwakiutl Culture as Reflected in Mythology* (New York: G.E. Stechert & Co., 1935). Wilson Duff, *The Upper Stolo Indians of the Fraser Valley, British Columbia* (Victoria: British Columbia Provincial Museum Dept. of Education, 1952; Duff "The Fort Victoria Treaties."

26 See Christopher McKee, *Treaty Talks in British Columbia: Negotiating a Mutually Beneficial Future* (Vancouver: UBC Press, 1996); Christopher McKee *Treaty Talks in British Columbia: Building a New Relationship* (Vancouver: UBC Press, 2009), Andrew Woolford, *Between Justice and Certainty: The British Columbia Treaty Process* (UBC Press, 2005); Duff "The Fort Victoria Treaties"; Edmonds, "Unpacking Settler Colonialism's Urban Strategies"; Harris, *Landing Native Fisheries*; Harris, "A Court Between."

27 Cole Harris, "How Did Colonialism Dispossess? Comments from the Edge of Empire," *Annals of the Association of American Geographers* 94, 1 (2004), 170.

28 Horne, "W̱SÁNEĆ: Emerging Land or Emerging People."

Barton's *Rethinking Scientific Literacy*.[29] The following story originally appeared in a paper for the Institute of Ocean Sciences in Sidney, BC:

> Once, long ago, the ocean's power was shown to an unsuspecting people. The tides began rising higher and higher than even the oldest people could remember. It became clear to these people that there was something very dangerous about this tide [...]. The seawaters continued to rise for several days. Eventually the people needed their canoes. They tied all of their rope together and then to themselves. One end of the rope was tied to an arbutus tree on top of the mountain and when the water stopped rising, the people were left floating in their canoes above the mountain. It was the raven who appeared to tell them that the flood would soon be over. When the flood waters were going down, a small child noticed the raven circling in, the child began to jump around and cry out in excitement, "NI QENNET TTH W̱SÁNEĆ" "Look what is emerging!" Below where the raven had been circling, a piece of land had begun to emerge. The old man pointed down to that place and said, "That is our new home, W̱SÁNEĆ, and from now on we will be known as the W̱SÁNEĆ people." The old man also declared, on that day, that the mountain which had offered them protection would be treated with great care and respect, the same respect given to their greatest elders and it was to be known as LAU, WEL, NEW—"The place of refuge."[30]

29 Wolff-Michael Roth and Angela Calabrese Barton, *Rethinking Scientific Literacy* (New York: Routledge, 2004).

30 Kevin P. Paul as quoted in Roth and Calabrese Barton, *Rethinking Scientific Literacy*, 41.

This story illustrates two things. First, the oral tradition traces the presence of W̱SÁNEĆ Peoples on what is now called the Saanich Peninsula to a time that is comparable to the biblical flood of Noah's Ark. Second, the territories on what is now called the Saanich Peninsula, and specifically what is now called Mount Newton (ȽÁU WELṈEW̱), were never viewed and treated as property to be bought, owned, or sold. ȽÁU WELṈEW̱ is a sacred place today and is still used for ceremonial purposes and the cleansing practices mentioned in *Rethinking Scientific Literacy*. The question remains: Why would W̱SÁNEĆ people sell something they considered to "be treated with great care and respect, the same respect given to their greatest elders"? They would not. It simply would not happen.[31]

The story of the Douglas Treaty of 1852, signed by Captain James Douglas and the signatories from the W̱SÁNEĆ Nation, and how this related to the supposed selling of our sacred ȽÁU WELṈEW̱ is an interesting one. The treaty came under question when a company wanted to dredge Tsawout Bay in order to build a marina. The government challenged the validity of the treaty for several reasons. First, the Treaty of Waitangi had recently been completed in 1840, and so the script was taken word for word, with "Waitangi" simply replaced with "W̱SÁNEĆ." Next, the signatories (all male, which is problematic for a whole host of other reasons) were listed by their English names and next to the English names were Xs, supposedly inscribed by the signatories themselves (including my great-grandfather, Etienne Smith). But each of the Xs was identical and therefore had been inscribed by the same hand. Finally, the entire treaty process was conducted in English and the treaty written in English, which was problematic because at the time English was not a language commonly used by the W̱SÁNEĆ people. Ultimately, the W̱SÁNEĆ (the Tsawout to be specific) successfully defended the treaty in court, and did so only to protect Tsawout Bay.[32]

31 Horne, "W̱SÁNEĆ: Emerging Land or Emerging People."
32 Horne, "W̱SÁNEĆ: Emerging Land or Emerging People."

The W̱SÁNEĆ Elder interview tapes I was given access to during the writing of my article for *The Arbutus Review* were recorded in preparation for a court appearance to protect Tsawout Bay. The Douglas Treaty designated only land within what is now called the Saanich Peninsula. It left out important fishing areas in the surrounding waters and vital resource gathering areas found on the surrounding islands. However, an example of the allegiance W̱SÁNEĆ feel toward our territory can be found in the marina court case excerpt taken from "W̱SÁNEĆ: Emerging Land or Emerging People," which states:

> In 1983 the Province of British Columbia issued a license of occupation to Saanichton Marina Ltd. in order that they could construct a marina and breakwater in Saanichton Bay. Traditional Tsawout fishing and resource gathering encompassed the entire of Saanichton Bay since time immemorial. In defense of this traditional fishery, the Tsawout peoples had been working to stop the construction from the time that the proposal was made public. In 1987 the British Columbia Supreme Court granted a permanent injunction for Claxton et al. against Saanichton Marina Ltd. The situation became a standoff, when in 1985, dredging began on the site, and Earl Claxton Jr. attached himself to the dredge cable, refusing to come down. For over an hour he stayed on the cable, while the freezing rain turned to sleet, until finally the two sides agreed to a [sic] halt the dredging until the court decided the matter. Claxton's actions were a testament to W̱SÁNEĆ attachment and dedication to traditional territories. In 1989 the Supreme Court once again sided with the Tsawout and the Saanichton Marina Ltd. project was permanently stopped.[33]

33 Horne, "W̱SÁNEĆ: Emerging Land or Emerging People," 11.

The dubious Douglas Treaty with the W̱SÁNEĆ Nation represents just one of many detrimental aspects of colonization of the British Columbia area.

The resettlement of British Columbia by European populations occurred in a drastically different way from the colonization of most of the rest of North America. Sustained contact with outsiders was effectively prohibited by the formidable Rocky Mountains for many years. In the two hundred years since European contact, Indigenous cultures all across British Columbia have been irrevocably changed. Contact was made by the Russians to the North, the Spanish to the South, and the British and Americans to the East. Many historians have found little evidence that these early fur traders had any interest in land settlement during the early contact period of the late eighteenth to mid-nineteenth centuries.[34] However, eventually the fur traders set up trading posts, and as the years progressed, there was an influx of non-Indigenous Peoples along with a drastic population decrease in many Indigenous Nations.[35]

As a result, the attitudes toward the original inhabitants began to change.[36] According to Cole Harris, the imposition of colonialism on the rest of what came to be called British Columbia did not require treaties.[37] A more honest history challenges colonial notions of a country "founded on nonviolence."[38] As settler colonies spread, the basis for the relationship between Indigenous and non-Indigenous Peoples shifted from one of trade to one of land acquisition. There was a movement toward creating reserve lands, dispossessing Indigenous Peoples, and acquiring territory needed for settler colonies, often using intimidation and force. Harris has

34 Duff, "The Fort Victoria Treaties."

35 Horne, "W̱SÁNEĆ: Emerging Land or Emerging People."

36 Duff, "The Fort Victoria Treaties"; Harris, *The Resettlement of British Columbia*.

37 Harris, *The Resettlement of British Columbia*, 4.

38 Paulette Regan, *Unsettling the Settler Within: Indian Residential Schools, Truth Telling, and Reconciliation in Canada* (Vancouver: UBC Press, 2010).

demonstrated that after a few public hangings and/or the shelling of a few villages in order to instill fear, it was "judged sufficient to anchor a Warship just off a native village and ostentatiously prepare the guns."[39]

Once the Indigenous populations were diminished by disease and the population of settlers increased, a mere show of force was enough to dispossess Indigenous nations of their land. The Oregon Treaty was signed in 1846, without consultation with any Indigenous groups. This treaty was an agreement between Great Britain and the United States, and established the border between what is now Canada and the United States. The border extends west from the mainland and veers through the Gulf Islands and around the southern tip of Vancouver Island. The signing of the Oregon Treaty, combined with the discovery of gold on the Fraser River, encouraged the government of Canada to establish a colony on Vancouver Island. Fort Victoria had been established in 1843, and the colony of Victoria was then established in 1849.[40] James Douglas, of the now infamous Douglas Treaties, was the governor of Vancouver Island (1851–1864) and of the mainland colony of British Columbia (1858–1864) at the same time. Douglas acted on behalf of the Hudson's Bay Company and was appointed by the British government as its representative to negotiate the transfer of ownership of Indigenous lands to the Crown. He made fourteen agreements with Indigenous nations from Victoria, Nanaimo, and Fort Rupert.[41]

Traditional embodied W̱SÁNEĆ Knowledge, however, extends far beyond those non-Indigenous written treaty concepts. The deep connection and commitment to living in harmony with W̱SÁNEĆ territories is demonstrated by the W̱SÁNEĆ flood story as well as

39 Harris, "How Did Colonialism Dispossess?," 169; Horne, "W̱SÁNEĆ: Emerging Land or Emerging People."

40 Duff, "The Fort Victoria Treaties."

41 Duff, "The Fort Victoria Treaties"; Horne, "W̱SÁNEĆ: Emerging Land or Emerging People."

the swift response of the W̱SÁNEĆ Peoples to the proposed marina in the Tsawout Bay. Both highlight the deep connection and commitment the W̱SÁNEĆ Peoples have to our territory, and demonstrate the longevity of our relationship to W̱SÁNEĆ spaces and knowledges. This is central to understanding my conceptual approach.

In *As We Have Always Done*, Leanne Betasamosake Simpson articulates the connection between Indigenous Knowledge and place:

> Years later, when I would begin thinking and writing about Indigenous resurgence as a set of practices through which the regeneration and reestablishment of Indigenous nations could be achieved, the seeds those Elders planted in me would start to grow with a strong *feeling*, more than thinking, that the intellectual and theoretical home of resurgence had to come from within Indigenous thought systems, intelligence systems that are continually generated in relationship to place.[42]

Similarly, the editors of *Indigenous Knowledges in Global Contexts*, define Indigenous Knowledge as:

> [A] body of knowledge associated with the long-term occupancy of a certain place. This knowledge refers to traditional norms and social values, as well as to mental constructs that guide, organize, and regulate the people's way of living and making sense of their world.[43]

42 Leanne Betasamosake Simpson, *As We Have Always Done: Indigenous Freedom Through Radical Resistance* (Minneapolis: University of Minnesota Press, 2017), 16.

43 George J. Sefa Dei, Dorothy Goldin Rosenberg, and Budd L. Hall, eds., *Indigenous Knowledges in Global Contexts* (Toronto: University of Toronto Press, 2000), 6.

I know that W̱SÁNEĆ X̱ÁLE: TOWARD A W̱SÁNEĆ KNOWLEDGE would be impossible without my deep connection with the W̱SÁNEĆ territories (land and sea), W̱SÁNEĆ oral and written narratives, exposure to W̱SÁNEĆ longhouse traditions, and all my W̱SÁNEĆ relations—both those living, and those who have moved on.

I think that the primary focus and responsibility of engaging in respectful Indigenous research is best articulated by Shawn Wilson:

> One major difference between the dominant paradigms and an Indigenous paradigm is that the dominant paradigms build on the fundamental belief that knowledge is an individual entity: the researcher is an individual in search of knowledge, knowledge is something that is gained, and therefore knowledge may be owned by an individual. An Indigenous paradigm comes from the fundamental belief that knowledge is relational. Knowledge is shared with all of creation.[44]

I have been conducting W̱SÁNEĆ theory from the first day my mom brought me to one of our longhouse gatherings and I participated in a practice referred to as the "basket dance." The basket dance is an integral part of the initiation ceremony undertaken to become a traditional W̱SÁNEĆ longhouse dancer. This was arguably the first instance of my embodying traditional W̱SÁNEĆ Knowledge. Such knowledge is embodied through interrelationships with W̱SÁNEĆ territory, places of spiritual significance, past and present practices on the land and sea, W̱SÁNEĆ oral narratives, relations to our ancestors, and our ancient longhouse practices. The relationality inherent in researching Indigenous Knowledge is a key component for me. It is also *the* major issue facing Indigenous research in the academy. Margaret Kovach articulates how "[r]elationship is not identified as a specific theme because it is wholly

44 Wilson, *Research is Ceremony*, 176.

integrated with everything else. Indigenous epistemologies live within a relational web, and all aspects of them must be understood from that vantage point."[45] In other words, there is an undeniable connection between ethical and true Indigenous scholarship and the concepts of relationality and accountability. By focusing through a lens of W̱SÁNEĆ ȾÁLE (heart), I avoid producing work devoid of W̱SÁNEĆ heart.

This writing, founded on traditional W̱SÁNEĆ Knowledge, has developed through my personal journey as an artist and academic. Accordingly, that journey has informed its design and focus. Here, traditional W̱SÁNEĆ Knowledge is explored through autoethnography, an example of which is the previously mentioned "basket dance" from our longhouse ceremonies. An additional method for gathering traditional W̱SÁNEĆ Knowledge was story-gathering. Margaret Kovach states that "[t]he conversational method aligns with an Indigenous worldview that honours orality as means of transmitting knowledge and upholds the relational which is necessary to maintain a collectivist tradition."[46]

Her statement highlights an important distinction, connecting relationality and accountability with the collectivism of traditional W̱SÁNEĆ Knowledge. Kovach's use of the conversational method in a group setting was not applicable to my work. However, the ideology described above was extremely useful, albeit in a much narrower application I refer to as the *visiting* method. Because story gathering for this writing was done within the specific W̱SÁNEĆ family group to which I belong, and at the time was conducted solely with my cousin Lola Garcia, any type of interviewing or sharing circles would have been far too formal and forced. Instead, my cousin Lola and I met on numerous occasions, and rather than

45 Margaret Kovach, *Indigenous Methodologies: Characteristics, Conversations, and Contexts* (Toronto: Universiity of Toronto Press, 2009), 57.

46 Margaret Kovach, "Conversational Method in Indigenous Research," *First People's Child and Family Review* 5, 1 (2010) 42.

taking notes and recording our conversations, we did what we always do as a family—we visited and talked. This is how it was done before written words, and before recording devices. We were the recording devices, and we are the archives.

The W̱SÁNEĆ Nation includes five large family groups. In the past, individuals have married into our Nation; however, this has never altered the knowledge and/or the demarcation of the original groups. Within each of the family groups, there are designated Knowledge Keepers, and my cousin Lola Garcia is one of them. Lola was trained to become our family Knowledge Keeper in the traditional W̱SÁNEĆ manner. Her mom (my Aunty Georgie) began taking Lola to gatherings at a very young age. At these gatherings Aunty Georgie would explain the protocol of each event or ceremony, and she would identify who the main participants were and what their function was within the W̱SÁNEĆ governance structure. It is important and significant to note that these gathering were always conducted in our traditional language of SENĆOŦEN. Lola informed me that when there was/is important work to be done within the W̱SÁNEĆ community, or when the W̱SÁNEĆ Nation experiences some sort of conflict, the heads of the families would call a meeting. The Knowledge Keepers, along with the heads of the families, would discuss and settle any W̱SÁNEĆ business according to established protocols. The current and past protocols are maintained through the oral history practiced by our Knowledge Keepers. In this way, there is consistency in the W̱SÁNEĆ governing structure. This also highlights the important position and concomitant responsibility my cousin Lola has within the W̱SÁNEĆ Nation. Lola shared with me how at times the Elders would share old stories at these meeting as one method of disseminating W̱SÁNEĆ oral history. The Knowledge Keepers would then be expected to take these stories and share them within their respective family groups. My cousin holds many of these stories, and it is these stories that she has generously shared with me.

One of the main issues when conducting Indigenous research is what to do when researching Indigenous Knowledge that is considered sacred. There have been a great many unauthorized depictions of sacred Indigenous Knowledges written by both Indigenous and non-Indigenous writers. Owing to my personal ethics as a W̱SÁNEĆ researcher, and the fact that my research involves a close working relationship with W̱SÁNEĆ Knowledge Keeper Lola Garcia, I am comfortable in writing about the previously mentioned aspect of our longhouse practice called the "basket dance" in the broadest of possible contexts. Writing of this practice is intended to illustrate one of the earliest memories I have, which involved embodying W̱SÁNEĆ Knowledge, without delving into specifics or making "exotic" one of our sacred practices. From the time I was very young, my mom made sure to instill in me and my family the principle that, as W̱SÁNEĆ people, we never discuss our longhouse practices with outsiders. W̱SÁNEĆ ethics, relationality, and accountability prevent specific descriptions of the origins and/or uses of practices such as the basket dance. My *accountability* as a W̱SÁNEĆ longhouse dancer and the voice of my mom preclude any notion of violating this vital protocol. I have read some startlingly accurate accounts of our longhouse practices, and I am aware that some ethical guidelines such the *Tri-Council Policy Statement: Ethical Conduct for Research Involving Humans* guidelines would allow for the use of those written accounts.[47] However, my own personal, familial, and W̱SÁNEĆ ethics do not.

During my visit home in December 2016, my cousin prefaced several stories with the words "This is for your ears only," and it was understood that any story following these words was not meant for anyone outside of the W̱SÁNEĆ Nation. Accordingly, I have no intention of speaking about them in any public gathering, seminar, or public presentation. Nor have any of those stories been

47 Government of Canada, I. A. P. on R. E. (2020, February 19). *Tri-Council Policy Statement: Ethical Conduct for Research Involving Humans*, TCPS 2 (2018).

included in this book. I am aware of the curiosity and appetite for sacred Indigenous Knowledges in the academy, but personal ethics take precedence.

This research explores the concept of embodied W̱SÁNEĆ Knowledge and the role it once played in traditional W̱SÁNEĆ Knowledge transfer. It further explores how embodied W̱SÁNEĆ Knowledges can be utilized in contemporary artistic and academic work. Research within the W̱SÁNEĆ Nation has required the development of a W̱SÁNEĆ-focused approach and the incorporation of what Māori theorist Linda Tuhiwai Smith terms "community research" methodology. Smith's methodology is meant to avoid what Indigenous scholar Adam Gaudry calls "extraction methodology," in which "[t]he extraction approach to research involves removing knowledge from its immediate context and presenting it to a highly-specialized group of outsiders."[48] Writing about traditional embodied knowledges, Leanne Betasamosake Simpson notes: "[o]ur bodies collectively echo the sounds of our ancestors, the sounds of the land, and (o)debwewin, the sound of our hearts."[49] Here I explore how these echoes form the key components of embodied W̱SÁNEĆ Knowledge, and by extension explore how I, as a W̱SÁNEĆ artist and academic, can facilitate embodied W̱SÁNEĆ Knowledge transfer using contemporary performance studies theory and theatre practices.

As a W̱SÁNEĆ artist, a W̱SÁNEĆ academic, and a W̱SÁNEĆ community member, I felt and feel a great responsibility. I feel a responsibility to ensure that my work remains focused on conducting research that is by, about, and for W̱SÁNEĆ Peoples and does not simply follow prescribed institutional demands. I understand the history and need for university ethics reviews, but from

48 Adam Gaudry, "Insurgent Research," *Wicazo Sa Review* 26, 1 (2011) 113, 114.

49 Leanne Betasamosake Simpson, "Bubbling Like a Beating Heart": Reflections on Nishnaabeg Poetic and Narrative Consciousness," in *Indigenous Poetics in Canada*, Neal McLeod, ed.. (Waterloo, ON: Wilfred Laurier University Press, 2014), 110.

a W̱SÁNEĆ perspective, the protocols surrounding the review and acceptance of my dissertation work from the W̱SÁNEĆ Nation and from my family always took precedence. Shawn Wilson writes: "[t]his becomes my methodology, an Indigenous methodology, by looking at relational accountability or being accountable to *all my relations*."[50] I agree with Wilson when he identifies relationality as a major part of an Indigenous methodology. It has always been my desire to further W̱SÁNEĆ scholarship, and that is the drive behind my work. Relationality and accountability to the W̱SÁNEĆ Nation forms the backbone of my research, which, as noted, focuses on the concept of embodied W̱SÁNEĆ Knowledges.

SX̱I¸ÁM (STORYTIME)

There are ȽḴÁĆES (five) SX̱I¸ÁM sections interspersed throughout this book. Each SX̱I¸ÁM was specifically chosen and strategically placed to demonstrate W̱SÁNEĆ Knowledge and to elaborate on my position and my journey through postsecondary education. Ultimately, each SX̱I¸ÁM serves as a marker illustrating through story my mental, emotional, physical, and spiritual health during this educational journey. The individual SX̱I¸ÁM also serves as an introduction to the chapter that follows it. The SX̱I¸ÁM are inscribed in various formats taken from unpublished plays, book manuscripts, and one even recounts a dream taken from a journal entry.

NEȾE (One) introduced us to SWÍ¸ḴE and her family as they gather seafood on the beach of one of our TETÁCES.[51] NEȾE is an introduction to pre-contact W̱SÁNEĆ living and is used as an example of written story, which is then deconstructed. This SX̱I¸ÁM precedes the introduction. In the introduction the reader is introduced to my research, early W̱SÁNEĆ research, and the research focus and structure. ĆESE (Two) centres on the character

50 Wilson, *Research is Ceremony*, 177.

51 Relatives of the deep (Islands)

of Frank Lafortune as he wakes in the Victoria, BC detox centre known as Eric Martin. This SX̱I,ÁM illustrates what it is like to live as an Indigenous person in the contemporary world and the perils of existing while connected to both the past and present. ĆESE precedes a chapter focused on my positionality as a researcher. In this chapter, the reader is introduced to the educational experiences of my parents, followed by my journey through postsecondary education. ĆESE also serves as a literature review in a storytelling format.

The ȽIW[52] SX̱I,ÁM leads into the chapter establishing a W̱SÁNEĆ paradigm. ȽIW̱ begins with SWÍ,ḴE, only now she has become SYÁ,TEN,[53] having lost her husband and family. This story highlights the strength and perseverance of the W̱SÁNEĆ Peoples as it tells the story of how SYÁ,TEN discovered the beautiful W̱SÁNEĆ village of WJOLEP. ȽIW precedes the W̱SÁNEĆ paradigm section and begins by detailing how the W̱SÁNEĆ women were the catalyst in the development of what is now called the Saanich Indian School Board and all the benefits attached to the SISB. None of it would be possible today were it not for the strength and foresight of the W̱SÁNEĆ women. The W̱SÁNEĆ paradigm section then moves on to articulate the challenges I had with one aspect of the Indigenous Studies PhD program at Trent University and ends by articulating the parameters of an Indigenous, and more specifically a W̱SÁNEĆ, paradigm. Finally, ȽIW introduces the reader to embodied W̱SÁNEĆ Knowledge and the connections between that and traditional W̱SÁNEĆ living.

ṈOS (four) introduces us to Muriel Miguel and the Spiderwoman Theatre's Storyweaving Performance Methodology. The SX̱I,ÁM preceding this chapter is very special to me. It was a dream that came to me during a very difficult period while I was still at Trent University and living in Peterborough, Ontario. I was recounting the dream to my supervisor Marrie Mumford, and I started to cry because I was just so tired. I was tired of fighting to have my voice

52 Three
53 Widow

and vision as a W̱SÁNEĆ person heard in academia. The W̱SÁNEĆ ancestors spoke to me in that dream and urged me to continue to reach forward with my whole heart and it is a memory I think of often. This SX̱I,ÁM has helped me to carry on through some dark times. W̱SÁNEĆ places and spaces are then used to deconstruct a performance piece I created titled *The Picnic* to illustrate a textual example of embodied W̱SÁNEĆ Knowledge and the intent of this project. The ȽḴÁĆES[54] SX̱I,ÁM precedes the final section of this book and acts as an introduction to the embodied W̱SÁNEĆ Knowledge transfer project *The Picnic* in its final form.

CONNECTING THE DOTS

The words that began this text introduced me in the traditional way, by also introducing my mom and dad. The prologue ends with a letter my mom wrote to me while I was still travelling, in which she expressed her concern over losing another Elder from the W̱SÁNEĆ community. My mom is the biggest reason why I undertook a dissertation, and the writing of this book, and much like the W̱SÁNEĆ women who are responsible for what eventually led to the current Saanich Indian School Board, she knew the importance of balancing W̱SÁNEĆ Knowledge with non-Indigenous learning. Of course, none of these women would have known the terms: systemic racism, cognitive imperialism, and academic gatekeepers. Those can change a beautiful journey full of support, learning, and growth into something filled with conflict, oppression, and trauma.

In the pages that follow, I detail my relationship to education and my journey through Camosun College, the University of Victoria, York University, and Trent University. Through this journey, I always held Indigenous and W̱SÁNEĆ research central in my academic writing. I have been unwavering in my determination to write as a W̱SÁNEĆ man and for the W̱SÁNEĆ Peoples. I have never had any interest in writing for the academy. By the time I ended up at Trent, I had an idea that I would teach Indigenous theatre, but never did I contemplate selling out and cutting myself off from my W̱SÁNEĆ Indigeneity to get there. This is what put me on a collision course with the academic gatekeepers at Trent University.

The Camosun College program featured mainly Indigenous instructors, and we read Indigenous scholarship. At the University of Victoria, the professors were mainly non-Indigenous, but they were committed to Indigenizing their classes by including Indigenous academic readings and encouraging Indigenous-focused writing. The Theatre and Performance Studies MA program at York University had almost zero Indigenous content and no Indigenous professors, and yet those professors were extremely interested in assignments written from an Indigenous perspective. I have heard that York University has since included more Indigenous content in its programs.

Trent University blindsided me and I was disappointed by the rigidity of the social sciences frameworks and rhetoric in the Indigenous Studies PhD program. The advertising for the Indigenous Studies department and PhD program touts the faculty's commitment to the Indigeneity of their classes and programs. Nowhere does it say any student entering their department or programs must submit to social sciences rhetoric. In fact, everything that drew me to the program touted a combination of Indigenous and non-Indigenous theory and methodologies. Somewhere along the line, this program lost its way, and by the time I arrived, the vision statement that originally drew me to the program was not adhered to at all when it came to the seminars led by non-Indigenous professors.

Here is a hypothetical for you to ponder. Say there is an Indigenous program started, and in the beginning, there are incredible Indigenous on-the-land practices mixed with the usual university pedagogy. The program leaders write a vision statement reflecting this. Now let's say a non-Indigenous professor joins the program and then stays with it for thirty years. Over the course of those years, the non-Indigenous professor becomes more senior and eventually takes over the entire program. This may be hypothetical, but this has happened over and over again in several universities across Canada and the United States. The reason this has happened so often is because in the early days of Indigenous Studies, there were few Indigenous professors and so naturally non-Indigenous professors filled those roles. This is not a problem provided the non-Indigenous professors do not alter the program to fit their non-Indigenous goals.

Now imagine you are a graduate student entering an Indigenous Studies PhD program touted as the longest-running such program in Canada. How exciting is that? Now imagine that the only seminar course in Indigenous Theory and Methodology is taught by a non-Indigenous person. This same person is also involved in every aspect of running the program, from who gets admitted to which grant applications are approved and make it out of the department for review. This means all applications must get approved by the committee with the non-Indigenous professor, and only those selected are submitted and leave the department. Those that are not selected are never seen by anyone outside of that department. What if this person was the one who ran the only core comprehensive exam preparation workshops for the department? What if the only writing retreat available for this Indigenous graduate student to attend was held at this same non-Indigenous professor's house every year over reading break? What if this Indigenous student was you and you did not get along with the non-Indigenous professor? What would you do? This non-Indigenous professor holds all the power and access to success in this hypothetical Indigenous Studies PhD program. That is messed up, isn't it?

After I had worked with the Centre for Indigenous Theatre summer intensive, I realized how vital that work was for empowering and educating the Indigenous youth. I immediately saw the utility of theatre as a vehicle for embodied W̱SÁNEĆ Knowledge transfer. The chapter articulating embodied W̱SÁNEĆ Knowledge examines embodied knowledge, embodied Indigenous and W̱SÁNEĆ Knowledge, and the Storyweaving performance methodology I experienced while working with Muriel Miguel at CIT. This became the focus of my research and ultimately led me to the question: How do I, a W̱SÁNEĆ artist and academic, use embodied W̱SÁNEĆ Knowledge in my artistic and academic work? I believe I have sufficiently answered that question in this writing.

The experiences I endured while studying and working at Trent University and in the years after I moved back to BC fundamentally changed me and my perception of the academy. In researching and writing my dissertation, I realized that my focus had shifted slightly. It was no longer solely embodied W̱SÁNEĆ Knowledge transfer. Instead, I began to question why it was so hard to carve out a space for embodied W̱SÁNEĆ Knowledge transfer in academia. This subtle shift in research foci then altered the research design so that my work became a case study of my journey through academia, along with the struggles involved in carving out a space for Indigenous Knowledge in the academy.

There are many wonderful aspects of the Indigenous Studies PhD program at Trent University and many of the professors, instructors, and staff were supportive during my quest to obtain a doctorate. This book is not meant as a wholesale critique or dismissal of Trent University, the Indigenous Studies department, or the Indigenous Studies PhD program at Trent University. I am telling my story, conveying my truth, and nothing more. Ultimately, I hope it will be read in the spirit that it was written—as a case study of one Indigenous person's experience.

X̱I,ÁM

(STORYTIME)

ĆESE

(TWO)

ERIC M.

Francis LaFortune (Frank) woke with a start to a red flashlight making an impressive array of patterns on the ceiling. There was a moment of confusion as he pulled himself from the hotel room and tried to remember where he was.

"Blood pressure check," the nurse whispered to the newest member of the ward.

Frank had already been here for five days and had gone through his own first night of interrupted sleep. Each new person went through the same routine, and so a new addition to the four-person room meant another round of "blood pressure checks" throughout the night.

Eric fucking Martin, he thought to himself. *What the actual FUCK?*

Anyone who had grown up in Victoria, BC knew about Eric Martin. The place was legendary to the point of becoming a verb: "Better be careful or they'll Eric M. you!" It was the place they sent the "crazies"—that notorious cousin who once stabbed a guy, or that too-friendly "aunty" that no one was allowed to talk about. Frank had had a moment of panic until the intake worker explained to him that a few years back they had redone the fifth floor of Eric M. and moved medical detox into the building. He figured it wasn't that far a stretch from addicts to the real nutjobs and thought that in fact the two groups had an alarming degree of overlap.

"Eric Fucking Martin," he whispered to himself as he rolled over and pulled the inadequate blankets up under his chin and tried to rearrange the two flat-ass pillows he'd stuffed into one pillowcase. The industrial-sized fan attached to the ceiling was impossibly loud, but he knew the importance of the apparatus. Five rooms held four detox patients each, and two rooms were singles. Each shared room had one industrial fan because there was only one bathroom per shared room. *One* bathroom for four people detoxing from alcohol, drugs, or both. Frank had made the mistake of voicing his concern about the inevitable diarrhea and one of the male nurses had said, "well when you come into this place, you kind of have to check that stuff at the door." Easy for him to say.

There were three ten-foot-high windows in Frank's room and his bed was next to the window. Rather than regular curtains, the windows had what reminded Frank of the old projector screens from his school days. It was the same vinyl material that had to be pulled down from the top. The vinyl curtains came down only so far, and Frank was sure they purposefully left an inch gap at the very bottom, which resulted in constant light coming in from the cold, empty parking lot below. The glass was single-paned, and this, combined with the industrial ceiling fan, meant a continuous draft of cold air throughout the night.

The Eric Martin building was located right next to Victoria's Royal Jubilee Hospital, which was the hospital where Frank had had his appendix out at the age of twelve. Eric M. and the RJH were situated at the outskirts of downtown Victoria, between the downtown core and the municipality of Oak Bay. Frank knew this area was traditionally shared territory for several of the local Indigenous Peoples: the Lekwamen, Lekwungan, Songhees, and his own W̱SÁNEĆ Nation. Ancestors treasured this area because of the massive old-growth cedar trees that used to grow in what was currently called Cadboro Bay. Because of the topography of the land and the natural protection afforded by the bay itself, the cedar trees grew incredibly straight and to impressive heights.

The nurse finished her intrusive duties, and Frank was left to listen to the loud industrial fan and the quiet snoring from the bed next to his. *Paved paradise and put up a parking lot*, he sang in his head, and smiled sadly as he stared at the desolate parking lot five floors down. The parking lot opened onto an intersection that was busy even at this hour. Looking down five floors, Frank could see where Fort Street and Cadboro Bay Road met. Going along Cadboro Bay would eventually lead a person to where the famous trees had once flourished, while heading the opposite direction would lead them to the heart of downtown Victoria. Frank knew that a mere two hundred years ago, this area would have been a pristine paradise. His people had been living in the area for much, much longer than a mere two hundred years. Time immemorial, in fact.

Frank smiled sadly again as he began to drift off.

RESEARCHER POSITIONALITY

In the article "Indigenous Research Methods: A Systematic Review," Alexandra S. Drawson, Elaine Tooms, and Christopher J. Mushquash "attempt to catalogue the wide array of Indigenous research methods in the peer-reviewed literature and describe commonalities among methods to guide researchers and communities in future method development."[1] A few of the Indigenous research methods those authors discuss were significant to my own research and writing. These methods included autoethnography, storytelling, conversational interviewing method, and a W̱SÁNEĆ-specific or, as articulated in their article, a *culture-specific* method.

This book uses what Drawson et al. term "mixed methods" in that "within Indigenous research, the term reflects a synthesis of the qualitative approaches that typify research with Indigenous Peoples and also unique Indigenous methods or ways of knowing."[2] An emphasis on Indigenous theories and methodologies along with a proposal for a W̱SÁNEĆ paradigm, in concert with the previously mentioned Indigenous research methods provide the solid

1 Alexandra S. Drawson, Elaine Tooms, and Christopher J. Mushquash, "Indigenous Research Methods: A Systematic Review," *International Indigenous Policy Journal* 8, 2 (2017), i.

2 Drawson et al., "Indigenous Research Methods," 5.

Indigenous research framework that I use in the creation of this work. Denzin and Lincoln write that:

> [q]ualitative research involves the studied use and collection of a variety of empirical materials—case study, personal experience, introspection, life story, interview, artifacts, and cultural texts and productions, along with observational, historical, interactional, and visual texts—that describe routine and problematic moments and meanings in individuals' lives.[3]

This description of qualitative research shows how diverse and open to possibilities it can be. Taking it a step further, Denzin and Lincoln also state that "[a]t this level, qualitative research involves an interpretive, naturalistic approach to the world."[4] However, according to Louis Botha, Indigenous research in the academy is most often not truly Indigenous. He notes that "[i]nstead, what passes for Indigenous research tends to be methods of data collection and analysis conducted and represented by westernized researchers according to modified, but ultimately hegemonic modern western knowledge traditions."[5] To mitigate this issue, my research was conducted with and through the lens of embodied W̱SÁNEĆ Knowledge. I used both Indigenous research methods/methodologies and those qualitative methods/methodologies most congruent with an Indigenous/W̱SÁNEĆ paradigm.

In their article "Autoethnography: An Overview," Carolyn Ellis, Tony Adams, and Arthur Bochner articulate several forms of autoethnography, including "personal narratives," which they assert propose "to understand a self or some aspect of a life as it intersects with a

3 Norman K. Denzin and Yvonna S. Lincoln, *The Sage Handbook of Qualitative Research* (Thousand Oaks: Sage Publications, 2005), 3.

4 Denzin and Lincoln, 3.

5 Louis Botha, "Mixing Methods as a Process Towards Indigenous Methodologies," *International Journal of Social Research Methodology* 14, 4 (2011), 213.

cultural context."[6] The authors also write that "[a] researcher uses tenets of *autobiography* and *ethnography* to *do* and *write* autoethnography."[7] I was first introduced to autoethnography as a graduate student at York University in the Theatre and Performance Studies MA program. D. Soyini Madison, and her work in South Africa introducing performance as an autoethnographic method of activism, had a deep impact. The scholarly writings of Dwight Conquergood were also an inspiration for my early research. However, a major drawback for most practitioners of autoethnography, in my estimation, is that most ethnographers must write from an outside perspective, as researchers studying the *other*. Luckily for me, my status as a member of the W̱SÁNEĆ Nation negated this major obstacle. This vital Indigenous connection, and the interrelationships it entails, are paramount for most Indigenous researchers studying our respective nations. Gregory Cajete writes in *Native Science*:

> Therein lies the difference between Western and Indigenous paradigms. The issue is a matter of perspective. Indigenous consciousness has always included, along with the practical relationships of the natural world, aspects such as the direct relationship of communities of people with the spirit of the place in which they have lived and the places they have come to know and understand.[8]

I respect the scholarship of Cajete, and I was very encouraged by his writing about the differences between an Indigenous paradigm and the western ones. This would become a source of major personal and academic conflict in my dissertation research, and with the Indigenous Studies PhD program that I chose to pursue.

6 Carolyn Ellis, Tony Adams, and Arthur Bochner, "Autoethnography: An Overview," *Historical Social Research / Historische Sozialforschung* 36 (2011), 7.

7 Ellis et al., "Autoethnography: An Overview," 1.

8 Gregory Cajete, *Native Science: Natural Laws of Interdependence* (Santa Fe: Clear Light Publishers, 2000), 78.

It would seem straightforward and obvious thus far that I had chosen to conduct research through a W̱SÁNEĆ lens. Unfortunately, the straightforward and obvious path to my dissertation would prove elusive. My life journey has played a significant role in my development as an artist and academic, and the challenges I have faced in my education have had direct correlation with my research choices. Ultimately, I have found that my personal ethics and commitment to the W̱SÁNEĆ Nation, and my concomitant obligations to my family, resulted in a deeply personal dissertation with a singular focus on advocating for embodied W̱SÁNEĆ Knowledge in the university system. It was my intention to avoid non-Indigenous theories, methodologies, and methods as much as possible and I was able to, for the most part. Where I had to utilize non-Indigenous researchers, it is obvious that their work supports my research; otherwise, I am clear about the reason for its inclusion. I have set this goal because I want to centre Indigenous/W̱SÁNEĆ Knowledge, and de-centre the hegemonic eurocentric whiteness regularly found, and repeatedly grappled with, in dominant social sciences university practices.

To articulate where I have ended up, we must first explore how I got here.

RESEARCHER EDUCATION JOURNEY

Education after colonization has been a delicate balancing act for the W̱SÁNEĆ Peoples. Soon after colonization, W̱SÁNEĆ children were either taken away to one of five residential schools located on or near to Vancouver Island, or they attended the Tsartlip Indian Day School. The day school was run by one priest and a few nuns. My parents each had different educational experiences, and it is important to explore these because they have a direct bearing on my life and relationship to education. I wish I knew more, but neither of my parents were very forthcoming about their early lives, and I am from the era where children respected their elders. If they did not offer an explanation, we did not pry. Over the years, snippets of information were shared, and we siblings eventually compared notes and were able to cobble together an incomplete story.

My mom never attended residential school, and neither did any of my aunts or uncles on that side of my family. Family legend indicates it was because my grandfather confronted the Indian agent at the end of his driveway with a shotgun. My grandfather told the Indian agent that if he came back and tried to take his children, he would kill him. It worked for the residential school, but it did not get my mom or my aunts and uncles out of attending the Tsartlip Indian Day School. My mom never talked much about her time at the school, other than to say the nuns who ran all the classes were mean. She was left-handed, but was forced to learn to write with her right hand. The nuns walked between the rows of desks during writing practice, and if they caught her attempting to use her left hand, they would rap her knuckles with a ruler. It was cruelly effective, because she had beautiful penmanship and I never saw her write with her left hand. My mom was an avid reader, and because this was something we shared, we often exchanged books. She had wide-ranging tastes, but she loved those cheesy westerns written by Louis L'Amour. My Mom never made it past the fifth grade.

My dad had a much harder upbringing. George Horne was born around 1930, and he was one of the last W̱SÁNEĆ people to practice SX̱OLE (reef net fishing) in the old way. The government made SX̱OLE illegal because it did not like that the W̱SÁNEĆ fishermen were catching so many salmon. Later, George Horne and the others became government-approved commercial fishermen, and this is the work he still does today. At an early age, he witnessed his parents' death in a boating accident, after which he was raised by a very strict uncle. One day, when he was about fourteen, some Indian agents showed up on the Tsawout reserve in a car and took him away to residential school. They did not even allow him to say goodbye to anyone or pack anything from home. To this day, I have never heard him speak about his time in residential school.

When my sisters and I were growing up, he refused to speak or allow my mom to teach us SENĆOŦEN, our language, because in his mind we were better off with English. This was a direct result of his time in residential school, and I sincerely regret never learning SENĆOŦEN. Both my mom and my dad were very focused on my success when it came to western education.

By the time I started attending school in the 1970s, Indigenous children had a choice of either attending the on-reserve Tsartlip Indian Day School or integrating into the Saanichton district school system. I was a quick study, learned to read early, and was good at math. What more does one need in the early days of western education? I did well and was always placed in the advanced classes. I discovered theatre and dance in high school, which would prove to be the start of a twenty-five-year career in the performing arts. That career was a great disappointment to my mom, because all I ever heard from her was that she wanted me to "get a degree"—she never elaborated beyond that. I started dancing at the age of seventeen, and by the time I graduated at nineteen, I knew I wanted to become a professional dancer. Unbeknownst to me, some of the teachers at my high school were attempting to obtain funding for me to attend Simon Fraser University with a scholarship in kinesiology. I dropped out of chemistry in grade twelve, and this meant I no longer qualified for the scholarship, but because I wasn't made aware of it at the time, it was not a big disappointment to me. I sometimes wonder what my life would be like now had I attended university in the 1980s. That was a time when Indigenous students were expected to write in third person and completely deny their Indigeneity. I would never have been permitted to write a dissertation in the first person. It is somewhat sad to think that yes, I was able use first person in my narrative by the time I did write a dissertation, but that some programs really have not progressed much beyond that. Despite my ability to use first person narrative, I was soon to discover that even in an Indigenous Studies program, there is still opposition to Indigenous Knowledge.

During my 25-year career in theatre, I worked hard and accomplished many things. I started working regularly in Vancouver and was cast in two big musicals under the direction and choreography of Jeff Hylsop, an icon in Canadian musical theatre. I also worked as an apprentice dancer for one year with the Judith Marcuse Repertory Dance Company of Canada. I moved to Toronto in the late 1980s to work with Rene Highway, and there I worked regularly with Rene, Alejandro Ronceria, and Raoul Trujillo. The four of us, along with Byron Chief Moon from Vancouver, were the only five Indigenous male dancers working in Canada at that time. I was in rehearsals for a production of *The Tempest* featuring Monique Mojica the year that Tomson Highway's *Dry Lips Oughta Move to Kapuskasing* (1989) won four Dora Mavor Moore awards. This was a historic moment for Indigenous theatre in Canada. Rene, a few other Indigenous performers from *The Tempest*, and I, crashed the awards ceremony at the Royal Albert Hall in Toronto, and that was when I first met playwright Tomson Highway. Rene was Tomson's younger brother. I'd had the fortune of working with Rene a lot before he passed away in 1991. I also did my third production of *A Chorus Line* (1977) and had a small speaking role in the TV movie *Conspiracy of Silence* (1993), about the murder of Helen Betty Osborne. It was in Toronto that I first auditioned for and was cast in a show on my first cruise ship. This would become a main source of employment for the next fifteen years or so.

I grew up isolated and poor on a reserve, and my lived experiences of the outside world were limited. Early in my career I managed to book two shows overseas. The first was a disaster of a tour in Spain and the second was a show in a nightclub in Nagoya, Japan. The shows were bad, and the choreography was terrible, but the experience of seeing other parts of the world was more than worth it. Later, when I began working on cruise ships, one of the biggest benefits was seeing the world—I loved it. Whenever I thought of leaving to do something else, I ended up getting offered a better ship with better shows and better itineraries. Over the years, I managed to visit most of the world, and along the way I met some amazing lifelong friends who I am still in contact with today. However, at the age of forty-two, I finally decided that I'd had enough. I had always intended to quit dancing one day and return to school. Initially, I set the date for my 30th birthday, and after my 30th birthday came and went, I changed it to 35. After the 35th, I decided to dance until I physically couldn't, or until they stopped hiring me. When I reached the age of forty-two and was still getting offered contracts, I finally made the decision to walk away.

I had been working and travelling the world since leaving high school. Many of my Indigenous friends had remained in Toronto and gone on to do some incredible work. This short section is not meant to be an exhaustive account of my performing career, but instead is meant to show my life path leading up to a return to post-secondary education in 2008. My first career and first love, theatre, was something I had no intention of continuing once I returned to school. I expected to focus on my studies, and therefore stopped everything associated with dance and theatre. I stopped teaching and taking dance classes so that my focus would remain on learning. It was a difficult choice, but I knew it was what I needed to do.

I had decided to walk away from performing once and for all and to pursue that degree my mom had advocated for ever since I'd learned to read. I had given up theatre and everything related to it, and now all that was left was to find a suitable program. When a funding application I submitted was approved, I began to seek out programs and through pure luck I discovered the Indigenous Studies program at Camosun College. I enrolled without any idea of how transformative this program, institution, department, and the staff and instructors would be in my life.

POST SECONDARY EDUCATION—THE RETURN

CAMOSUN COLLEGE YEARS: 2008–2010

My return to education started with the Native Studies diploma program at Camosun College in 2008. The program has since been renamed Indigenous Studies. I could not have picked a better program as a starting point for my academic journey. The Indigenous Studies program at Camosun fostered a safe learning environment, and the class instructors were very supportive and encouraging. I had been out of school for decades by that point, so writing for the academic environment became the biggest priority. I do not recall much of what I read except for Leroy Littlebear's "Jagged Worldviews Colliding".[9] This piece really resonated with me on multiple levels, primarily because it reminded me that I had spent decades working in theatre and traveling the world in some of the most beautiful places on earth, and in between jobs I would return home and visit my family. I witnessed my siblings starting their own families and all of them embracing our W̱SÁNEĆ traditions while I traipsed around the world dancing. It was a culture shock every time I went from one environment to the other.

I embraced Littlebear's writing because it was exactly what I needed to hear at a time when I felt lost. I had just left a career I loved and was successful at for twenty-five years, and I was searching for something to fill that void. I had attempted to attend university twice before, and both times I ended up returning to travel and dancing because that was where my heart was. I was not interested in the style of learning I encountered in university classes—the rote memorization of facts as a display of knowledge. I found it extremely boring. When at Camosun College I stumbled upon Littlebear's writing and discovered there was a different way of writing, and it filled me with hope. Littlebear's prose expressed why I felt so disconnected both when I returned

9 Leroy Little Bear, "Jagged Worldviews Colliding," in *Reclaiming Indigenous Voices and Vision,* Marie Battiste, ed. (Vancouver: UBC Press, 2000), 77–85.

home to visit family and when I returned to work sailing the seven seas. Equally importantly, his writing showed me the potential that Indigenous Knowledge and Indigenous scholarship have in the academy. I realized I was not alone in my jagged worldviews, and that it was okay to embrace that, because it could be used to speak my truth. This was an important epiphany for me, and I return to this piece of writing often because it reminds me of the moment when the importance of Indigenous scholarship revealed itself to me. Littlebear's writing showed me the power and potential of an authentic Indigenous voice in academic writing.

Unfortunately, my mom passed away suddenly the summer after my first year at Camosun. When I retired from theatre and returned to Canada, I moved in with Mom and my sister and we ended up spending a great deal of time together. We talked a lot about W̱SÁNEĆ traditions and about the ways that she remembered some of the issues I was studying at Camosun—Indian agents, for example. I regret that we did not have more time together and I often wonder at all the knowledge she must have held. My mom was the keystone in our family, and we all loved her deeply. Her sudden passing threw us into chaos, and we each struggled to find healing. I moved to Vancouver where I briefly worked for performing artist and artistic director Margo Kane, and Full Circle: First Nations Performance. During those three months, I was actively trying to drown my sorrow with alcohol. This is never the answer to grief, and I eventually had to return to Victoria to seek help. I secured a spot at Round Lake Treatment Centre, an Indigenous-based drug and alcohol facility in the interior of BC. I attended Round Lake in November of 2009, and then I entered one of our longhouses to become initiated as a traditional W̱SÁNEĆ new dancer in December 2009. Both experiences helped to smooth out some of my jagged worldviews and deepen the connection to my W̱SÁNEĆ Indigeneity.

When I returned to W̱SÁNEĆ territory, I began organizing Round Lake, my longhouse initiation, and the return to Camosun

College. The latter proved to be more challenging than I expected, but it was a testament to Camosun's willingness to work collaboratively on the issue. Camosun allowed me to return to classes while I was still considered a "new dancer" in our longhouse traditions. This meant there were protocols I had to follow. Camosun made room for those protocols, and I heard later that it prepared the other students—about half were non-Indigenous—with a meeting prior to my return. It was exhausting to attend classes during the day and then longhouse gatherings during the evenings, but I managed and was all the stronger for it. It showed me that the collision of two worldviews could be managed provided all parties were willing to educate and were open to fostering a safe and accepting learning environment. I can think of no better example of Camosun's commitment to honouring Indigenous Knowledge in education than the experience of returning to post-secondary classrooms while I was still considered a W̱SÁNEĆ new dancer. It proved that Camosun's commitment to a true Indigenous education environment was so much more than a performative vision statement thrown out when the college felt the need to affirm a commitment to Indigenous Knowledge in the academy. Camosun College demonstrated commitment with its actions, and those actions spoke much louder than any performative written statement.

There were many aspects of the Indigenous Studies diploma program at Camosun College that lent themselves to a safe and nurturing environment for Indigenous students. A cohort of students developed from each year and progressed together through two years of classes. Even when students were taking classes outside of the Indigenous Studies program, there were always members of the cohort there for support. Most of the instructors were Indigenous, as were most of the administrative staff in the Indigenous department offices. It was always comforting to have Indigenous role models instructing classes, or in positions to offer support when needed. Because of the proximity to the University of Victoria, we often had professors from the Indigenous Governance MA program come and give guest lectures. Dr. Jeff Corntassel and Dr. Taiaiake Alfred were two notable highlights. We were also fortunate to have many Elders from the surrounding nations either come in to give guest lectures, or our class would go out to visit the Elders in their territories. We hosted potlucks at Camosun College, attended sweats hosted on W̱SÁNEĆ lands, and gave end-of-term presentations at local community gathering places. It was a holistic learning experience, and I feel fortunate to have had this as my re-entry into post-secondary learning.

One beautiful spring day in 2010, a friend and I decided to walk over to the University of Victoria and tour the campus. We decided to explore the Indigenous offices located in the First Peoples House of Learning. While there, we visited with the academic advisor, and I discovered I was eligible enroll at the University of Victoria immediately and to take most of my credits from Camosun College as transfer credits. This all happened after my mom passed and I had attended Round Lake Treatment Centre. It was also after I was initiated as a W̱SÁNEĆ longhouse dancer. I made sure to consult with Elders and the staff and instructors at Camosun before I made the monumental decision to leave the Camosun diploma program and begin an undergraduate degree at the University of Victoria in the summer of 2010. I had been initiated into our longhouse traditions to honour my mom, and I could think of no better way to further honour her memory than by pursuing the degree she wanted for me all those years ago. I completed my final classes at Camosun in April 2010 and started with two political science classes at the University of Victoria in June 2010.

THE UNIVERSITY OF VICTORIA: 2010–2013

The change from Camosun College to the University of Victoria was a very drastic one, and the learning curve was steep. The first-year university lectures had anywhere from 30 to 150 students and the demographic of students skewed toward a younger population.

It seemed as if they were all straight out of high school and were laser-focused on what they wanted to study and why. It was incredibly intimidating, and I had to work hard to catch up. Because of the lectures I had attended at Camosun given by the directors of the University of Victoria Indigenous Governance MA program, I set my sights on acceptance to that program. I discovered that many of the students accepted into the Indigenous Governance program had done their undergraduate degrees in political science. That is why I decided to start my classes at the University of Victoria with two political science electives. In retrospect, I wonder what I was thinking, because I had zero knowledge of or interest in political science and yet this became my major. It was a challenge, but because I have always been keen on new knowledge, it was a challenge I ultimately enjoyed.

The University of Victoria had some world-class political science scholars in the department, and I did my best to take classes with as many of them as possible. Influential professors included Dr. Janni Aragon, Dr. James Tully, and Dr. Warren Magnusson. I appreciate professors who are obviously extremely intelligent and great educators who conduct themselves with humility and kindness. When it came to electives, the majority I chose were Indigenous Studies courses. The University of Victoria offers a minor in Indigenous Studies, but because I was attempting to finish my degree in three years, I was unable to complete said minor. Instead, I chose to spread out the remaining electives in as many areas of interest I could. Always eager to learn, I ended up taking many of my electives in sociology and women's studies. Regardless of the department or professors, during those three years at UVic, the professors teaching in all but one of my classes were open to written assignments from an Indigenous perspective. The one holdout class was international political economy—a difficult class I did my best to simply pass so that I could then move on to additional required courses for a political science major. In all other courses, the professors always included an assignment choice with

Indigenous content, or they encouraged students to incorporate Indigenous Knowledges if we desired. It was a fantastic learning environment, and one of the reasons Indigenous Studies at the University of Victoria is cutting edge.

One of the best and most useful aspects of the University of Victoria is the Native Student Union and a room dedicated to Indigenous students at UVic. The NSU is run by a committee of Indigenous students who are elected to their positions. This elected committee is responsible for developing and hosting events throughout the year, and for maintaining the Native Student Union lounge. The NSU lounge is located in the student union building and once I found it, I spent a great deal of time there. It had a row of computers with free printing, a couch and some chairs, a table, refrigerator, microwave, toaster, coffee maker, and electric kettle. Most times, there were snacks available. Once I did a walk by to see who was there and finally worked up the nerve to enter the space, I found that it was the best spot—an Indigenous oasis in the middle of academia. It was a great place for meeting Indigenous students from different departments at UVic. They were very free with advice about which professors and classes were most welcoming when it came to Indigenous Knowledges. It remains one of the places I remember with fondness because later institutions lacked this basic amenity.

The learning environment was very different from the one at Camosun college. I believe one of the reasons was that the Indigenous Studies department at Camosun knew that many of us were returning to school after an extended absence, or for the first time, and therefore they were gentle in their teaching approach and expectations. Additionally, in the Indigenous Studies diploma program at Camosun College, the students all attended the same courses and supported one another through all the classes. It was still hard work, but with the insulated, safe environment and the all-around support, the hard work was made bearable. Over at the University of Victoria, the learning curve was much steeper, and the environment veered toward individual success rather than group cohort success. Classes were spread out across multiple departments and across the campus in various buildings. There were many classes in which I was the only Indigenous student. This is one of the biggest challenges in post-secondary education; that isolation can be oppressive. I learned quickly that written assignment expectations varied between professors. Grading was often subjective depending on the positionality of the professor and therefore I adjusted my writing to match. I became less willing to do this in graduate school because I felt that at the more advanced level, we should be writing our truths and not be expected to mimic what we thought the professors wanted to hear. This is one of the issues that brought me to a breaking point during my time at Trent University. More on that later.

I am the first in my family to graduate from high school and a first-generation university student. I had no prior knowledge and no one to turn to for advice about how post-secondary education is supposed to work. All I knew was that I liked learning and I wanted to learn. Because I did not know any better, my process was to accept the grades given, learn from the written notes what it is I did wrong, and then correct it for the next assignment. Therefore, my grades always improved over the course of any given term. I have since learned that it is common practice to approach the professor and negotiate some sort of accommodation such as resubmitting a paper or rewriting an exam. It turns out that most professors are open to this practice, and it is routinely allowed. After all, they are not unfeeling robots, and many understand the pressures of taking four to five university classes at once. However, it was difficult for me to ask for something I considered special treatment, and because of the previously mentioned steep learning curve, I was not focused on improving on something I had already completed, especially given that there were always multiple new projects on the horizon. As a result, I almost never tried this. Now I realize how useful those higher grades are when it comes to grant applications, but back then, graduate studies were not even a consideration. The one thing I did get right, because it was often encouraged by the professors, was to write my assignments from an Indigenous perspective. By the time I left UVic in 2013, I knew that this was the future of my academic journey.

The reading I did at the University of Victoria was varied across departments. Not all of it was useful; however, the writings of Franz Fanon, Albert Memmi, Paulo Freire, Michel Foucault, and Linda Tuhiwai Smith were awe-inspiring and inspirational. Books that were more recent and covered in various Indigenous studies classes included Margaret Kovach's *Decolonizing Methodologies* (2009), Shawn Wilson's *Research is Ceremony* (2008), and Taiaiake Alfred's *Wasáse* (2005). Finally, during the years 2010–2013 while I attended UVic, several incredible publications came out which would become vital in the formation of my research. These included Eve Tuck and Wayne Yang's *Decolonization is Not a Metaphor* (2012), Leanne Betasamosake Simpson's *Dancing on Our Turtle's Back* (2011), and an article that I wrote in 2012, "W̱SÁNEĆ: Emerging Lands or Emerging Peoples," also became important to my future research. The Tuck and Yang article was inspirational because of its non-apologetic and forceful writing. It offered a tone and perspective I had not encountered before. This was a piece of academic writing written with Indigenous academics in mind. It was a difficult read for an undergraduate student, but well worth those early attempts. Simpson's book resonated, but the reasons for this would not become clear until much later in my education journey, after she had delivered guest lectures to our PhD cohort at Trent University. I include my own published article not because I think it is a great piece of writing, but because it represents the catalyst for my PhD dissertation research.

In those early years of my post-secondary education, I met quite a few instructors and professors who would become instrumental in guiding and developing my education goals. Dr. Todd Ormiston was the director of the Indigenous Studies program at

Camosun College, and he was very supportive and encouraging when I expressed an interest in moving from Camosun to UVic. Dr. Janni Aragon in the Political Science department at UVic gave me so much encouragement and support. Dr. Aragon led by example, was one of the most ethical people I ever met, and she helped me to become a better writer. Dr. Adam Gaudry was still a PhD candidate in the Indigenous Governance program when I first met him. Dr. Gaudry taught a third-year Indigenous Studies undergraduate course that I found challenging but so very engaging. It was in this class that I wrote a paper which he later encouraged me to submit to an upcoming *Arbutus Review* issue highlighting Indigenous undergraduates. It was while conducting the research for this article that I discovered the glaring lack of W̱SÁNEĆ scholarship in the library's collection. For example, when I searched the library catalogue for anything related to the Haida Gwaii Nation, the search yielded hundreds of thousands of results. Yet searching the same for anything related to W̱SÁNEĆ or Tsawout yielded 11 results. I did manage to find some interesting research that I included in the article, but in the end, there was almost no academic writing about the W̱SÁNEĆ Peoples, and I wanted to change that.

The article I wrote was published in the *Arbutus Review* in 2012 as I continued to work toward obtaining my BA the following year. It had been three years of hard work, but I was on track to graduate in the summer of 2013. I still did not have a clear idea of what I wanted to do next, and once again the Indigenous student advisor at the University of Victoria would provide me some direction. In 2010, approximately one year after my mom's sudden passing, I wrote a play titled *Indigenous Like Me* that was dedicated to my mom and her story. In it, I was able to incorporate my experiences as an Indigenous man in theatre, Mom and her story, and the university knowledge I acquired from Indigenous Studies and political science. I performed this play at Intrepid Theatre's YOUShow festival in November 2012 and it was a cathartic experience. The Indigenous advisor in the First Peoples House of Learning had gone to see the play and suggested that maybe this was something I should consider exploring for future education and career goals. Following up on this suggestion, I applied and was accepted to the MA in Theatre and Performance Studies at York University. The Indigenous student advisor at UVic, Crystal Siebold, altered the course of my life. I finished classes at the University of Victoria in the summer of 2013 and organized my move to North York in Toronto late August 2013.

YORK UNIVERSITY: 2013–2014

York University has a population of approximately 50,000 students, which is more than Camosun College and the University of Victoria combined. In September, the campus is teeming with students, and it is quite an overwhelming experience. I had lived in Toronto from 1989 to 1991 and I had travelled to some of the most populous areas of the world, so overcrowding was not the issue for me. York University is a city and community unto itself, with a definite institutional and colonial environment. I lived on campus in one of four high-rises dedicated to housing for York students. One of the advantages to living on campus was that there was no need to travel on the overcrowded city buses, especially during the winter, when the bus service became dicey. Instead, I could walk to class no matter how bad the weather got. Disadvantages included the many undergraduates in my building who were young and not always interested in learning, which meant the building could sometimes get noisy. Additionally, 2013 saw the worst winter in over a decade and included an ice storm that shut down campus for a week. None of this really made a difference to me because the MA Theatre and Performance Studies program had a massive reading component, and I spent every day reading from before sunrise until after dinner, and the weather outside was ultimately of little concern to me.

As a first-generation university student, I had some difficulty in adapting to undergraduate learning. After three years at the

University of Victoria, I had developed a good routine. When I moved to York University it became evident that I was not prepared for the change to graduate seminars, because I had no prior knowledge of how graduate studies worked. Once again, I was in a new environment and faced with learning a whole new set of rules, and once again, it was sink or swim. In retrospect, I really do not think there was any way around the sense of panic I felt in those first few weeks. No amount of research could have prepared me for it. York University has quite a good Indigenous student services office, but by the time I got around to visiting it, I had missed its yearly introductory meet and greet. Instead, I was busy setting up my apartment and making sure to obtain my U-Pass student card so that I could access the library and food services on campus. In the end my reading load was so high that I only visited those offices a handful of times over the year. My cohort for the year-long MA program was about ten graduate students. I was much older than most of the others, and of course the only Indigenous graduate student. My cohort was diverse, and we all had particular life and education experiences. A few members of the cohort had obtained their undergraduate degrees from the theatre department at York University, and therefore they had the advantage of already knowing some of the professors. They also had the advantages of prior knowledge of performance studies theory and an overall understanding of how York University's Department of Theatre and Performance Studies functioned. I, on the other hand, found myself having to learn a whole new language just to participate in the weekly seminars. The learning curve was steep, but I put in the time and eventually managed to get up to speed. I have never read so much in my entire life as I did during the twelve months that I attended York University.

Realizing that there was a great deal of important theatre and performance studies knowledge that I was missing, I met with various professors and the department chair so that I could solicit advice on extra readings. I was thankful for having learned to approach the professors and always grateful for the extra help offered during office hours. One of the things I noticed immediately at York was the lack of Indigenous content in the Theatre and Performance Studies MA program. It was at one of these office hours meetings where I was advised to include this observation in my program exit interview. York University, like many other universities across Canada, has since made it a priority to incorporate Indigenous content into its programs to Indigenize the academy. I applaud York University for its progress after I had moved on, but in 2013 I was left to my own devices. I continued to practice what I had learned at UVic, and I tried to write each assignment from an Indigenous perspective. The professors at York were very encouraging and welcomed this perspective rather than opposing me and trying to shut it down. They did not fear Indigenous Knowledge in the academy, perhaps because most theatre people are open to new experiences and inclusive of new or alternative ideas.

When I decided to complete my undergraduate degree at UVic in three years, it meant I had to take classes year-round. I remained in classes from the summer of 2010 through to the end of summer 2013. I then immediately moved from Victoria to North York in Ontario to start the one-year MA program at York University. I inevitably started to suffer academic burnout toward the end of the winter 2014 term as the academic load and the years of unending study caught up to me. I decided to meet with the York University MA Theatre and Performance Studies program chair to discuss extending my studies for an extra semester because I found that I was not enjoying the experience. I had lost all sense of learning, and it had become about surviving from one written assignment to the next. I thought that perhaps if I cut back on classes and took a few over the summer that I could pick up what I had missed in the fall. This way I thought I might rediscover the enjoyment in learning. After I met with the program director and a couple of professors, we agreed this was the best course. Just when I thought I could slow down and enjoy classes again, I received an email from

Trent University with an offer to attend the Indigenous Studies PhD program in the fall of 2014. I contacted the university immediately to ask if I could delay my entrance into the program until January 2015. I was informed that they could not hold a spot, and if I missed the September 2014 intake, I would need to reapply for the next year. There was no guarantee that I would be accepted the second time. I met with the department chair and the professors from three courses I was enrolled in to ask what I needed to pass the classes and graduate in time. In the end, I wrote three final papers within a two-week period. I passed all three seminars with very good grades and then completed two more seminars and an internship over the summer. I did not get the breather I had planned, but I did graduate and was eligible to begin the Indigenous Studies PhD program at Trent in the fall of 2014.

The sheer amount of reading I completed over the course of that year was astounding. I read constantly from before sunrise until dinner. All my free time was spent reading, and I had no social life beyond walking my dog. I learned so much in such a short period of time about performance studies, Black studies, education, cinema and media arts, and theatre history. I chose my electives outside of the Department of Theatre and Performance Studies because I wanted new perspectives and experiences. Again, I am always interested in learning new things–it is always about the knowledge for me. The performance studies readings I was inspired by included the work of Erving Goffman, Victor Turner, and Richard Schechner—the founders of performance studies theory. I saw the potential to use their theories in the exploration of where performance studies theory met W̱SÁNEĆ traditional practices. I continued to develop assignments from a W̱SÁNEĆ perspective, and the response from all my professors was encouraging. They found my work interesting because it was so different to what they were used to. I was also inspired by D. Soyini Madison's book *Acts of Activism: Human Rights as Radical Performance* (2010), which was written about South African performance art.

This work showed me the potential of theatre in activism and education. In Madison's inspirational book, the grassroots performers developed their voice through theatre and then educated their community members and outsiders about a wide range of South African social issues.

One of the final seminars I took was in the Department of Cinema & Media Studies, and the topic was archives. To be honest, I think I took it because it fit into my summer schedule, and I thought it might be an easy elective. This was not the case, and yet it remains one of the most important seminars I took, because it fundamentally changed the course of how I approached W̱SÁNEĆ research. The rest of the students in the class were the film school type, and they seemed to already have a great deal of experience creating their own film projects. They were an unbelievably intelligent group, and once again I found myself in an environment with its own culture and language. This time, I knew I was a temporary visitor and therefore I had no obligation to learn the lingo. I simply did my best to complete the readings and keep up with the discussions. The class focused on archives and archivists and how each were invaluable research tools and potential gold mines for artistic and academic projects. It was an interesting class, and the readings and lectures were engaging. We were encouraged to begin searching for an archive to utilize in the creation of our final projects immediately. I eventually settled on The United Church of Canada Archives in Toronto because the church archived residential school photographs. Over the course of the summer, I made two trips to downtown Toronto to conduct archival research, which was an interesting and sad experience.

Taking this seminar led to my discovery of *The Archive and the Repertoire* (2003) by Diana Taylor and resulted in a profound shift in my research focus. One of the seminar requirements was for each student to choose a week in which we were responsible for leading discussion about the readings. I choose this book because the synopsis piqued my interest and it mentioned that Diana Taylor was a

South American scholar. I also chose it because this book was the only option with Indigenous content in it. In recalling these events at York University, I am reminded of why this book and the related presentation experience marked a pivotal point in my academic journey. It is an example of how my jagged worldviews collided with those of other graduate students, both at York University and in academia generally.

The other graduate students were interested in learning the many ways the archives are a treasure trove of material for documentaries, museum exhibits, and academic research. They were interested in the ways the myriad of archived materials could benefit any future projects, and they seemed to be seeking best practices for obtaining access to them. There was a great deal of animated discussion when it came to the stories of those items "found" in an archive that had become lost for various reasons. The rediscovery of archival artifacts and the process of making them available to the public was a boon for researchers and often led to awards and grants. I will admit that even I was fascinated, because it was like finding lost treasure. However, I knew instinctively what Taylor's book meant from an Indigenous perspective because I knew W̱SÁNEĆ Knowledge did not have a written or an archival component. Therefore, our knowledge was held and conveyed in ways that were not archivable in the way that we had been studying in this seminar. I understood when Taylor made the distinction between the "archive" and the "repertoire" that W̱SÁNEĆ Knowledge was entirely the repertoire.

These concepts were new to me at the time, and beyond Diana Taylor's book I had done no additional research. I could only interpret her work through my jagged worldview of W̱SÁNEĆ Knowledge, and so it was limited. When my turn came to lead the seminar discussion and present Taylor's book, I made the mistake of speaking as if the other students and I shared the same perspectives or worldviews regarding knowledge. I spoke of the archive and the repertoire as written by Taylor, embodied knowledge and how W̱SÁNEĆ Knowledge was never written. I spoke of how our knowledge was not archivable, was not individual, but instead was a shared collective knowledge. Once I finished speaking and looked up, I saw nothing but blank faces staring back at me with confusion. Then came a barrage of questions that I sincerely wish I had recorded because it would have been so applicable for this writing. I recall only a few of the questions because I was confused by my fellow students' reactions. I remember they asked, "If its not written down, where is it kept?" and "what do you mean embodied? Like in the arm or leg?" They could not grasp or accept the idea of collective knowledge that was not tangible and could not be locked away in a box. The idea of knowledge anywhere outside of a book was incomprehensible them. It was fascinating to me, and remains one of the most interesting university experiences that I had, though the reality of the situation would not become clear to me until much later, after I had left York University. My final residential school project included a digital story I created. It went over very well, and I received an A in that class.

As noted, my initial plan was to take an extra semester to complete my MA at York University and then to apply for a doctorate there. I saw the potential in the meeting of W̱SÁNEĆ Knowledge and performance studies theory, and this seemed like the best educational path. The acceptance email from Trent disrupted that plan and I had to make a choice. The lack of Indigenous content in the MA Theatre and Performance Studies program at York University played a huge part in my decision. I fully expected that attending an Indigenous Studies PhD program at Trent University would mean an environment that respected and encouraged Indigenous Knowledge in research. Trent's vision statement for the Indigenous Studies PhD program led me to believe this was the case. Therefore, it seemed to me that a return to Indigenous Studies would complete the education circle I started at Camosun College. In the end, I finished my summer courses at York University and moved my life to Peterborough, Ontario to begin the next stage of my education.

TRENT UNIVERSITY: 2014–2023

My journey through life and the academy was like a winding path twisting through the woods. Because I had no clear destination and seemed to always be in unfamiliar territory, the readings I engaged with were done on an as-needed basis for the classes I was taking. This served to expand my general knowledge in whichever discipline I happened to be studying, in addition to those readings that piqued a particular area of interest. The latter were usually Indigenous-related. But once I arrived at Trent, I began to zero in on *my* area of PhD research and so the readings naturally became more focused. It remained my intention to centre Indigenous Knowledge and Indigenous writers in my work. Where using non-Indigenous work, I was, and still am, always clear about the reasons. Usually it is because that research has not yet found its way into the Indigenous Studies field, and it is the work of scholars who write in opposition to knowledges commonly accepted in the ivory tower and/or the gatekeeping practices of some university professors.

Prior to arriving at Trent University, I had been fortunate to study under supportive and nurturing instructors and professors. I had managed to avoid those in the academy who were not open to Indigenous or alternative knowledges. If I found myself in a class or seminar where the professor was ignorant of other pedagogies, I knew I could produce work they would approve of, as I had done so on many occasions. However, when I left York University to attend Trent University, it was because I expected that in an Indigenous Studies PhD program, I was going to be able to continue to produce scholarship through Indigenous theory and methodologies in a context where these concepts would be understood. And I expected that at the doctoral level, I would have the academic freedom to do Indigenous, and specifically W̱SÁNEĆ research.

The day I sat in the library at the University of Victoria, discovered the lack of research materials available about the W̱SÁNEĆ

Nation, and decided to change that, was the genesis of my doctoral research. How to go about accomplishing this task became the ultimate challenge in my academic journey. I want my writing to be accessible to the W̱SÁNEĆ Peoples—a goal that placed me in conflict with a few key individuals in the Indigenous Studies PhD program at Trent University, and demonstrates where I think they get their vision statement twisted. The vision statement, as it was written in 2014, was a primary reason why I was drawn to the Indigenous Studies PhD program at Trent. I discovered in my first term that what the institution expected from program participants was not at all what its vision statement promised. The statement promised a respectful environment in an Indigenous program grounded in Indigenous knowledges and Indigenous community. It also promised both traditional and contemporary Indigenous Knowledges, yet what I discovered was a focus on social science paradigms taught aggressively by a non-Indigenous professor. I immediately came into conflict with the white professor because our jagged worldviews collided, and the uneven power dynamic allowed for oppressive bullying tactics to be employed. The way this was done suggested to me that I was not the first Indigenous student to experience those tactics. This proved to be the beginning of two and a half years of trauma I experienced while on campus at Trent.

The Indigenous Studies PhD program at Trent University had a large core comprehensive reading list. The 106 books were divided into the following categories: Traditional Knowledge (Canada and Internationally), Indigenous Knowledge/Thought/Orality, Language, Discipline of Native Studies/IK and the Academy, Governance/Self-Government/Sovereignty, Lands and Spaces, Research Inquiry and Ethics, Indigenous Advocacy: Activism, anti-colonialism, resistance, and resurgence, and Other Critical Perspectives.

Trent recently narrowed the core comprehensive reading for the program down to a list of seventy titles. The newer list has been revised and updated to include many contemporary Indigenous scholars. Core comprehensive reading lists are meant to contain the core knowledge from any given field that students are expected to demonstrate a mastery of in both written and oral exams. Looking back, I believe that Trent's Indigenous Studies PhD program list attempted to include too many older readings and books. Some of this material should have instead been assigned as seminar readings rather than kept on the core list. This would have made room for more contemporary works in the developing Indigenous Studies field. But in 2014, this was the content of our reading list regardless of how it came to be configured, so I set about reading.

I am not the type of student who can read the first and last chapter of a book to get a rough idea of the content and then move on, and neither can I read the first couple of paragraphs and then the conclusion of an academic paper. I read everything because I have an obsessive need to learn and to digest as much information as possible. Therefore, if the list I am given has 106 books on it, I am going to do my level best to read 106 books. I did not read every book and article on the list because there were a few that either had no significance to me as a researcher, or the subject material had zero interest to me personally. I attempted to read N. Scott Momaday's *House Made of Dawn* (1966) three separate times, but I just did not understand why it was on our core comprehensive reading list. Similarly, I had no interest in Dale Turner *This is Not a Peace Pipe* (2006) or Paul Rabinow's *The Foucault Reader* (1991). It became evident to me that as Indigenous scholars we are expected to read and engage with non-Indigenous scholarship throughout our early academic journeys. Therefore, it is my opinion that we shouldn't have to continue to do so in graduate studies unless our research requires it. Chances are we have already encountered much of the material already. For example, I read Turner's book back at UVic and I studied Foucault there as well, in the political science program. I knew there was no need to revisit either.

A required first-year course in the Indigenous Studies PhD program at Trent University was titled Graduate Seminar in Indigenous Theory and Research Methods. Based on the title of the seminar alone, I had anticipated Indigenous-focused readings. Instead, we got a white professor teaching almost exclusively social sciences theory and methodologies taken from social science paradigms. I did what I had done at every other institution and attempted to conduct my research and writing from an Indigenous and W̱SÁNEĆ perspective, but I found that these efforts were discouraged using verbal rebukes and low grades for assignments written from those perspectives. In response, I began to do my own research and discovered a shocking lack of Indigenous writing on the topic of Indigenous research in the academy. At the end of the first year, I asked if I could submit a final paper on this topic to make up for a missed presentation, and the professor permitted me to do so.

I ended up dividing the core comprehensive reading list into two categories. The first category was for readings that I read just because they were assigned in a seminar, and I knew were a part of the core list for comprehensive exams. The second category was for readings that I found useful for my own research as well as for the core comprehensive exams. I read through the lens of my own research, with the knowledge that I would be using them in my dissertation work. I was interested in Indigenous scholars and their writing that intersected with embodied Indigenous Knowledge. Embodied Indigenous knowledge has been written about by Indigenous scholars prior to the genesis of the field of Indigenous Studies. Concepts have long been articulated regarding Indigenous Knowledge as it relates to Indigenous songs, stories, ancestors, land, and spiritual places. The importance of relationality, in addition to how the ancestors have had and continue to have input into this method of knowledge gathering and knowledge transfer, is key to embodied Indigenous knowledge. In his book *The People and the Word*, Indigenous literature scholar Robert Warrior has this incredible insight:

> Embodied discourse that relies on memory does not always or even primarily rely on language and speech

> acts. Many actions in Native life are neither primarily oral nor even linguistic, such as ceremonially presenting someone with provisions, taking part in a ritual fast, being part of a societal dance, or cooking a communal meal. All these actions can have complex levels of meaning within the confines of Native tradition, but those meanings are not necessarily best elucidated by textualizing them.[10]

Diana Taylor and Robert Warrior each define embodied Indigenous Knowledges in the most interesting and relevant of ways. Taylor lists the non-written aspects of spoken language, dance, sports, and ritual, while Warrior takes it one step further to include non-spoken acts such as cooking a communal meal or other public and private group activities. Our knowledges are encoded into these activities and transferred from generation to generation. When interpreted from these perspectives, embodied Indigenous Knowledge yields vibrant and interesting results.

According to Willie Ermine in "Aboriginal Epistemology," the difference between Indigenous and non-Indigenous research is that the latter strive for *objective* inculcation of knowledge whereby the researcher is separate and therefore *fragmented* from the knowledge gathering process.[11] Compartmentalization of Indigenous Knowledge leads to the problem of *fragmentation* found in standard western research methods. Gregory Cajete presents the Indigenous perspective in *Native Science*:

> The Native American paradigm is comprised of and includes ideas of constant motion and flux, existence consisting of energy waves, interrelationships, all

10 Robert Warrior, *The People and the Word: Reading Native Nonfiction* (Minneapolis: University of Minnesota Press, 2005), xxix.

11 Willie Ermine, "Aboriginal Epistemology," in *First Nations Education in Canada: The Circle Unfolds*, Marie Battiste and Jean Barman, eds. (Vancouver, UBC Press, 1995).

> things being animate, space/place, renewal, and all things being imbued with spirit.[12]

The key word from my perspective is the *interrelationships* of knowledge gathering and knowledge transfer found within Indigenous ontologies and epistemologies. I highlight Cajete's casual use of the phrase "Native American paradigm," as this concept becomes important to my analysis.

Past Indigenous scholars have been expected to engage with Indigenous Knowledge from the Western academic perspective. This has meant engaging from an objective, fragmented place. Fragmentation results in compartmentalized scholarship such as that found in Donald Fixico's "Oral Tradition and Traditional Knowledge."[13] In this chapter of his book, *The American Indian Mind in a Linear World*, Fixico examines the category "story" from an interesting and telling perspective. He compartmentalizes it and then reveals how story relates to the categories of land, spirituality, language, and Ancestors. The result is that Fixico westernizes the concept of story by first isolating it and then relating it to the other categories of embodied Indigenous Knowledge, when in fact all five categories are interrelated in such a way that they all blend into one another. It is this fragmented western eurocentric academic format that my research seeks to avoid.

While conducting this early reading I found there was another, more extensive category of reading that involved material specifically chosen for my own research. As my dissertation research became more directed, it grew and shifted over time. There was also an unavoidable correlation with events happening to me at Trent University that affected what I read and why. In June of 2015, Universities Canada released "Universities Canada Principles on

12 Cajete, *Native Science*, x.

13 Donald L. Fixico, *The American Indian Mind in a Linear World: American Indian Studies and Traditional Knowledge* (New York: Routledge, 2003).

Indigenous education."[14] Ninety-seven universities put forth thirteen recommendations for improving the recruitment and retention of Indigenous students and suggestions for fostering a university environment that is safer and more accepting for Indigenous students. While it is laudable for these universities to have put forth these recommendations, it is obvious from the problematic language that this short announcement represents the perspectives and goals of the universities, and not the voices of the oppressed Indigenous students. Despite the statement that these principles have been "developed in close consultation with Indigenous communities," there are no citations of, nor any other indication of just which communities were consulted. The research I did for a final paper submitted in April of 2016 revealed that every single one of the thirteen proposed recommendations put forth by the Universities Canada announcement had already been addressed by numerous Indigenous scholars in academic work which dated back for *decades!*

One of the most prolific and respected of those scholars is Dr. Marie Battiste. In "Enabling the Autumn Seed: Toward a Decolonized Approach to Aboriginal Knowledge, Language, and Education," Battiste criticizes the education process for Indigenous people and quite harshly critiques institutional eurocentrism: European exceptionalism and worldviews centered on western concepts.[15] I see eurocentrism as the view by which western theory and methods are perceived by the academy to be the only legitimate place from which legitimate scholarship can be derived. Indigenous students are expected to write from a western

14 Universities Canada, "Universities Canada principles on Indigenous education," https://univcan.ca/media-room/media-releases/universities-canada-principles-on-indigenous-education/#:~:text=Recognize%20the%20importance%20of%20indigenization,faculty%2C%20professional%20and%20administrative%20staff.

15 Marie Battiste, "Enabling the Autumn Seed: Toward a Decolonized Approach to Aboriginal Knowledge, Language, and Education," *Canadian Journal of Native Education* 22, 1 (1998).

positionality regardless of their personal, political, or Indigenous orientation. Battiste states:

> Eurocentrism is not like a prejudice from which informed peoples can elevate themselves. In schools and universities, traditional academic studies support and reinforce the Eurocentric contexts and consequences, ignoring Indigenous world views, knowledge, and thought, while claiming to have superior grounding in Eurocentric history, literature, and philosophy.[16]

Battiste then engages the question of why any critique of eurocentrism (and I use the lower-case deliberately), can

> raise anguished discourse about knowledge and truth. As questions are raised about alternative ways of knowing and diversity, the discussion quickly slips into paradigm maintenance by supporters for the Eurocentric cannon. Thus Eurocentrism resists change while it continues to retain a persuasive intellectual power in academic and political realms.[17]

The use of the term "Native American paradigm" by Cajete and here by Battiste, highlighting eurocentric resistance through *paradigm maintenance*, and the eurocentric foundation that has been hindering the progress of Indigenous Knowledge in the academy, began to reveal itself to me through these readings. In her work, Battiste goes on to discuss how we as Indigenous scholars and educators need to be cognizant of these problems as we decolonize our own practices. She advocates for healing by acknowledging our own worldviews and using this as the starting point for the future of Indigenous research.

The Battiste paper is combative, and was written at a time when Indigenous acceptance in the academy had barely made any

16 Battiste, "Enabling the Autumn Seed," 22.
17 Battiste, "Enabling the Autumn Seed," 23.

progress. I admire Battiste and her courage for publishing this in 1998, and I wonder at the backlash she surely received. Battiste's entire career has been dedicated to furthering Indigenous educational progress in academia, and for that I am grateful. In 2002, she co-wrote "Decolonizing Education in Canadian Universities: An Interdisciplinary, International, Indigenous Research Project" with Lynne Bell and L.M. Findlay. The article was the most detailed examination of the progress toward including Indigenous Knowledge in the academy that had been made to that point. It offers some interesting and inspiring insights as well as the usual critiques of academic eurocentrism:

> For those of us who have been educated in colonial, Eurocentric environments and had our Aboriginal identities revised or our white armor polished, we have needed to unpack Eurocentric processes to reveal the cognitive assimilative regime that has done such damage and what can be done to effectively change it.[18]

I remind the reader that at the time I encountered this article, I was engaging in extra reading because I found an alarming lack of Indigenous content in the Indigenous research course in the Indigenous Studies PhD program at Trent University. This article affirmed the discomfort I had been feeling during that first-year, two-semester seminar.

I had come to Trent University and the Indigenous Studies PhD Program specifically because I wanted to return to Indigenous Studies and to focus on W̱SÁNEĆ research. I was not prepared for what happened because I was instead besieged by eurocentric western research theory and methodologies. I knew that what was occurring was wrong, but as a first-year PhD student, there was little I could do other than to meet with the department chair and

18 Marie Battiste, Lynne Bell, and L.M. Findlay, "Decolonizing Education in Canadian Universities: An Interdisciplinary, International, Indigenous Research Project" *Canadian Journal of Native Education* 26, 2 (2002), 90.

express my concerns. I tried to explain that as a PhD student I had already spent six years at four different institutions engaging with western research paradigms, and I had hoped that when I came to Trent, that I might be able to move beyond those paradigms and write the way that I wanted. My concerns were noted, but I was repeatedly told that that was just the way it was in the Indigenous Studies PhD program at Trent University.

I knew these issues were not unique to Trent University because I had connected with many Indigenous academics on social media, and I heard similar stories about multiple programs and institutions. I was however surprised that, considering its reputation, Trent's Indigenous Studies program would be so narrowly focused on eurocentric western research paradigms, and that when I attempted to address the issue, I was completely stonewalled. Trent University was unique in this regard because at every other institution I had attended, I was encouraged to engage with Indigenous Knowledge in my research and writing, whereas at Trent, I found that any attempts to bring an Indigenous perspective in discussions and writing were shut down or rebuked. The atmosphere became very combative, and that is no way to nourish and engage any student.

In 1991, Verna J. Kirkness and Ray Bernhardt wrote "First Nations and Higher Education: The Four R's—Respect, Relevance, Reciprocity, Responsibility." In this piece, the two writers examine the lack of representation of Indigenous Students in colleges and universities in Canada and the United States and offer suggestions for addressing these issues. It is a combination quantitative/qualitative article, and one of the few quantitative articles I have enjoyed. The two scholars discuss the difficulties Indigenous students encounter when entering the environment of the academy, and point out the low retention rates that most institutions achieve. They articulate the problems and failures found at most institutions in creating equal education opportunities and safe environments for Indigenous students. Then they pose the following challenges for academic institutions:

If we are to address this perennial issue in a serious manner, we have to ask ourselves some hard questions:

- Why do universities continue to perpetuate policies and practices that historically have produced abysmal results for First Nations students when we have ample research and documentary evidence to indicate the availability of more appropriate and effective alternatives?
- Why are universities so impervious to the existence of *de facto* forms of institutionalized discrimination that they are unable to recognize the threat that some of their accustomed practices pose to their own existence?
- What are some of the obstacles that must be overcome if universities are to improve the levels of participation and completion of First Nations students?[19]

This was published in 1991, and there I was attending an Indigenous Studies program in 2014—twenty-three years later—and finding these same questions still applied. Not only was I surprised by the seeming lack of progress that had been made integrating Indigenous Knowledge in the academy, but I was also surprised at the lack of scholarship on this subject written by Indigenous people. Through my research, I discovered that that the 2016 Universities Canada announcement not only borrowed some of these scholars' writing, but that it then did not even cite these Indigenous scholars' work. It was obvious to me where Universities Canada had found their thirteen recommendations and I was disappointed in their lack of scholarly ethics.

One of my favorite discoveries deconstructs the differences found between Indigenous and non-Indigenous perspectives in the academy and does so with razor-sharp insight. Bryan McKinley Jones

19 Verna J. Kirkness and Ray Barnhardt, "First Nations and Higher Education: The Four R's—Respect Relevance Reciprocity Responsibility," *Journal of American Indian Education* 30, 3 (1991): 1–15.

Brayboy and Emma Maughan wrote "Indigenous Knowledges and the Story of the Bean," which centres on an Indigenous Teacher Preparation Program (ITPP) held at Western University at the end of two summer sessions.[20] One of the authors is Indigenous and the other non-Indigenous, and the balance of both points of view is evident in their writing. During their writing process, Brayboy and Maughan maintained constant interaction through formal and informal meetings with both faculty and students, in addition to weekly sessions with both. At one of the final meetings as the summer sessions wound down, the students were asked what they thought of the program thus far. One Indigenous student referred to the faculty and support staff as Mickey and Minnie Mouse because of their propensity to speak quickly and use academic jargon. This invariably made the students think that the faculty were more interested in impressing themselves rather than in making actual connections with or educating the Indigenous students. In their piece, the two authors astutely comment on how this "implicates the epistemic clashes inherent in how knowledge is used and how hierarchies of knowledge are produced and reproduced," and how "[t]hese clashes raise critical connections between power and the (re)production and transmission of knowledge."[21] Academic jargon and the strict use of western theory and methodologies can be tools for the continued oppression and alienation felt by many Indigenous students.

The portion of article that I found the most interesting and entertaining was the "Story of the Bean" from which the title is taken. One of the requirements for the Indigenous students was to assist in a teaching environment where they were assessed by site teacher educators (STEs) based on a rubric provided by the university. In

20 Bryan McKinley Jones Brayboy and Emma Maughan, "Indigenous Knowledges and the Story of the Bean," *Harvard Educational Review* 79, 1 (April 2009): 1-21.

21 McKinley Jones Brayboy and Maughan, "Indigenous Knowledges and the Story of the Bean," 2.

one of those teaching environments, the STE was concerned that their Indigenous teaching assistant was not ready to teach because she felt this Indigenous teaching assistant did not understand the curriculum. The curriculum of concern was for a Grade 4 class and had as an exercise a classroom of students planting seeds—one in soil and the other in sand. The Grade 4 students were then tasked with measuring different amounts of water for each in addition to keeping track of the plant growth. They measured the plant growth with a ruler and were responsible for keeping track of these results in a journal. The idea was for the Grade 4 students to experience the way scientists conduct an experiment. The learning outcomes for this exercise were math through the measurement of water during watering, and in calculating the plant growth. The students also developed writing skills through the act of journaling. It was meant to be a very straightforward exercise typical of most curriculum for students of that age.

The STE felt that her Indigenous student teacher was not ready to teach in the classroom environment, and was prepared to fail her. That would have meant the Indigenous student teacher would not have been able to obtain her teaching certificate. At a meeting with faculty, students, and STEs, the Indigenous student teacher was asked what she thought of her teaching curriculum and her experience of working as a teaching assistant. Her response was a perfect example of approaching pedagogy from an Indigenous Knowledge perspective. The Indigenous student teacher replied that the class curriculum as it had been structured was not the way she would have taught the lesson. She then proceeded to lay out how, working from a holistic Indigenous perspective, she would have taught a lesson in plant growth. She started by clarifying that she would never have planted seeds for no reason—meaning she would not have wasted the plants nor the labour by planting something knowing it was just for show. She also mentioned that it was a waste of time to plant seeds in the sand because everyone knows that seeds do not grow as well in sand, so that part of the experiment was unnecessary. The Indigenous teaching assistant then proceeded to lay out her vision of an Indigenous lesson plan in plant growth. The first thing she said she would do is to remove the lesson from the classroom and take it outdoors where the plants naturally exist. The lesson plan would begin by teaching the students about the many different plants and their seeds. She envisioned teaching the students how and when the different plant seeds were meant to be planted and teach them that in the traditional Indigenous way this was done when the stars aligned in a specific way. The Indigenous student teacher's lesson would also include the traditional stories which contained the Indigenous Knowledge about the stars, the plants, and the seasons for planting. It was amazing to read how this experiment went from an in-classroom exercise with no real purpose to a real-world exercise in different seeds, the time of year to best plant them based on the stars, and their uses along with their traditional stories. Of course, the STE became very interested in the proposed Indigenous lesson plan.

This article articulates numerous key insights regarding Indigenous Knowledge in the academy and helped to address reasons for my growing discomfort in the Indigenous Studies PhD program at Trent. I was inspired by the way ontological and epistemological Indigeneity were allowed to function once the lesson was removed from the usual colonial classroom setting and students were potentially allowed to become engaged through an Indigenous perspective. I saw how this process would allow the students and the teacher to engage with the outside world instead of the usual learning typically done stuck inside a classroom. It is important to recognize at all levels of teaching and learning, from kindergarten through to graduate studies, that there are valuable alternative ways to go about these goals. Indigenous ways of being and knowing have value and eurocentric western theory and methodologies should never be the only option; they should certainly never be forced upon an unwilling student. The Brayboy and Maughan article gave me an idea of the way that conducting W̱SÁNEĆ research might look as opposed to what we were studying in the Indigenous Research Theory and Methods seminar. We spent an inordinate amount of time studying theory and methodologies grounded in social sciences paradigms. My cohort spent a couple of weeks on grounded theory alone, and another couple of weeks going through Trent's online application for ethics review. So rather than spending time on the previously mentioned books and articles that engage with issues of Indigenous students and Indigenous Knowledges in the academy, we were instead made to spend much of our time on the very reason engaging with Indigenous Knowledge in the academy and Indigenous student success remains a struggle in academia in the first place. That being, the continued hegemony of western eurocentric research, grounded in social sciences paradigms in the academy in general, and its continued dominance in the field of Indigenous Studies specifically.

Dr. Marie Battiste wrote a report for the National Working Group on Education and the Minister of Indian Affairs: Indian and Northern Affairs Canada (INAC) titled "Indigenous Knowledge and pedagogy in First Nations Education: A Literature Review with Recommendations."[22] The report contains some very critical statements directed at education institutions in Canada, and focuses on the prevailing eurocentric western mindset. However, the report mainly advocates for the uplifting and acceptance of Indigenous Knowledge in research and the academy. The reference list and the appendix of annotated Aboriginal education resource materials alone are invaluable for Indigenous researchers. However, for the purposes of my work, Battiste's writing about literature reviews is most relevant:

> [I]n the European (or Eurocentric) knowledge system, the purpose of a literature review is to analyze critically

22 Marie Battiste, "Indigenous Knowledge and Pedagogy in First Nations Education: A Literature Review with Recommendations," National Working Group on Education and the Minister of Indian Affairs: Indian and Northern Affairs Canada (INAC), 2002.

> a segment of a published topic. Indigenous knowledge comprises the complex set of technologies developed and sustained by Indigenous civilizations. Often oral and symbolic, it is transmitted through the structure of Indigenous languages and passed on to the next generation through modeling, practice, and animation, rather than through the written word. In the context of Indigenous knowledge, therefore, a literature review is an oxymoron because Indigenous knowledge is typically embedded in the cumulative experiences and teachings of Indigenous people rather than in a library.[23]

This is an extremely important concept and highlights one of the most persistent obstacles to the acceptance of Indigenous Knowledge in the academy and in graduate research: the idea that knowledge is only acceptable if it comes in book, or written, form. There is complete lack of understanding or acceptance of Indigenous Knowledge and its nature, because it is collective and embodied, and as Diana Taylor writes, it is not archivable. Battiste's report is invaluable because it critiques the western academic complex while also advocating for Indigenous Knowledge and offering potential solutions.

Jeff Corntassel wrote a surprisingly funny academic article titled "An Activist Posing as an Academic?" in which he exposes some of the dangers of working as a junior academic within the university environment.[24] Corntassel tells a personal story about an interview he had for a tenure track position where he was accused by the interview committee of lacking objectivity. He writes that "[b]y refusing to apologize for being a Tsalagi professor, I practiced

23 Battiste, "Indigenous Knowledge and Pedagogy in First Nations Education," 2.

24 Jeff Corntassel "An Activist Posing as an Academic?" *The American Indian Quarterly* 27, 1&2 (2003): 160-171.

the academic freedom that these scholars lauded publicly but suppressed privately."[25] This reminded me of the unease I felt at the thought of an ethics board reviewing my proposed research conducted on the W̱SÁNEĆ Nation and with *my* family and community. The idea that this more than likely all non-Indigenous ethics committee would decide whether to grant me permission to do this research seemed unnecessary and oppressive. I understand the need to make sure all research that is conducted by students is done ethically. However, it is my own personal W̱SÁNEĆ ethics that take precedence. As an Indigenous and W̱SÁNEĆ man, this is first and foremost in my mind. Unfortunately, the Trent ethics requirements only represented hoops I needed to jump through, and nothing more. Corntassel sums it up nicely: "[r]ather than adopting a 'walking in two worlds' philosophy, I was Tsalagi first and foremost."[26] While I wholeheartedly agree with the sentiment of walking in two worlds and I acknowledge the necessity and benefits of being able to navigate both the Indigenous/W̱SÁNEĆ world and the world of academia, my allegiance has always and will always be to my W̱SÁNEĆ community and family *first.* One vital reference Corntassel shares is from an unnamed Cherokee/Cree professor who laments, "I thought we already fought these battles. You're fighting the same damn battles that we fought in the 1970s."[27] This is very interesting to me, because the articles I reference in this chapter were written in the 1990s, but can still be applied to the academy today. Obviously, there has been a great deal of progress and there is a demonstrable dearth of academic work from which current academic research can be drawn. My point however, is that the dominant narratives so jealously guarded by the academy are still creating eurocentric barriers for Indigenous academics, and professors are effectively still strong-arming graduate students into writing in the accepted eurocentric western formats.

25 Corntassel "An Activist Posing as an Academic?,"161.
26 Corntassel "An Activist Posing as an Academic?," 179.
27 Corntassel "An Activist Posing as an Academic?," 166.

I will offer one final example of Indigenous research in the academy before moving on to alternatives to western eurocentric theories and methodologies. No discussion of this subject would be complete without including the incredible work of Linda Tuhiwai Smith and her husband Graham Smith. In my opinion, the Indigenous researchers from New Zealand are ahead of those in Canada when it comes to carving out a space for Indigenous Knowledge in the academy. I first became aware of Professor Graham Smith at Camosun College in the Indigenous Studies program. The director of Camosun's program, Todd Ormiston, regularly met and corresponded with Professor Smith when Smith acted as an advisor/mentor for Ormiston on his PhD dissertation. Smith's wife and academic partner Linda Tuhiwai Smith's *Decolonizing Methodologies* is probably on every reading list for every Indigenous education course in the world, and rightfully so. Tuhiwai Smith published her book in the UK and the US in 1999, so her research and writing for the book was likely conducted more than twenty years ago. In it, she advocates for an engagement with dominant theory but from an Indigenous perspective. It's important to be aware that this was at a time when Indigenous voices in the academy were almost unheard of. In a chapter about Kaupapa Māori research, she engages with concepts like critical theory and positivism while exploring the ways that Māori research engages, relates to, and pushes back against them. More recent research work advocated by Professor Graham Smith and subsequent writing by Linda Tuhiwai Smith indicate a movement away from this type of engagement and towards a transformative praxis. My aim is not to provide an exhaustive examination of the writings of two professors Smith, but instead, to examine their early works that contributed to the burgeoning field of Indigenous Studies.

Professor Graham Hingangaroa Smith gave a keynote address to the Alaskan Federation of Natives Convention in Alaska in 2003, titled "Indigenous Struggle for the Transformation of Education and Schooling." In the talk, Smith advocates for avoiding what he terms the "politics of distraction" so that as Indigenous people we can experience "the freeing of the indigenous mind from the grip of dominant hegemony."[28] He provides several lists articulating ways to reach this goal under the headings: "The need To Centralize the Issue of Transformation," "A Call to Theory," and finally "Kaupapa Māori Theory." Smith's keynote focuses on the ways Indigenous communities can transform themselves through the detailed lists. What was most important for me was Smith's point that "[t]he term 'decolonization' is a reactive notion; it immediately puts the colonizer and the history of colonization back at the 'centre.'"[29] I first heard of this concept as an undergraduate when Dr. Taiaiake Alfred gave a talk where he advocated for a movement away from colonizing language and toward transformative and/or resurgent ones.

Smith similarly advocates for the continued development of Indigenous-focused research and "to position our own ways of knowing as being relevant and significant in the 'elite' knowledge production and reproduction 'factories'," and how we must have an "understanding of the politics surrounding theory, the understanding of the flaws of theory and academic work of the past, and most of all, the proactive development of indigenous theorizing by ourselves."[30] Smith considers the struggle between the academy and Indigenous communities to be only one part of the overall picture. He argues transformative work focused on Indigenous communities must also be done. This is significant because Smith does not advocate for the usual engagement with western theory and methodologies, but instead for the development of our own individual Indigenous theory and methodologies. Smith does not use

28 Graham Hingangaroa Smith, "Indigenous Struggle for the Transformation of Education and Schooling," The University of Auckland, Keynote Address to the Alaskan Federation of Natives (AFN) Convention, Anchorage, Alaska, 2003, para 2.

29 Hingangaroa Smith, "Indigenous Struggle for the Transformation of Education and Schooling," para 3.

30 Graham Hingangaroa Smith, "Indigenous Struggle for the Transformation of Education and Schooling," para 5, 1.

the word paradigm, but ultimately an Indigenous paradigm would accomplish his goals.

In response to certain aspects of the PhD program at Trent University my research focus and learning were altered as I felt necessary. When I discovered the paucity of written materials about the subject of Indigenous Knowledge in academia, and the subsequent problems this created for Indigenous students in the academy, I needed to learn more.

When I returned to British Columbia, there was a great deal of introspection and healing that I needed to do. Over the course of four years, I moved from Ontario to Victoria, and then moved from there to Vancouver, where I currently reside. Though it was incredibly difficult, I never stopped doggedly pursuing my research. At a fundamental level I had lost all focus and drive, and yet I persisted in my research and writing. I managed to successfully complete the core comprehensive written exam in August of 2018, and then I successfully defended my dissertation proposal in February 2020, right at the beginning of the COVID pandemic in British Columbia. The four years between 2017 and 2021 were full of incredible successes and devastating failures. I viewed it as one of the times in my life where I was forced to fight for what I believe in. Eventually, 2021 proved to be the year that I finally made significant strides in my research and writing. The first step in accomplishing this was to address the issues that I'd encountered in the Indigenous Studies PhD program at Trent University. Doing this meant engaging with dominant paradigms to establish the existence of an Indigenous and/or W̱SÁNEĆ paradigm. This proved to be an interesting but difficult and time-consuming task.

SX̱ I¸ÁM

(STORYTIME)

LĪW̱

(THREE)

LELILEṈ[1]

SYÁ¸TEN[2] woke well before sunrise and turned over to make sure ḴAḴ[3] was sleeping before rising to start her day. She stirred the embers in the fire pit and added fresh wood ĆEḰ,I,U,SE,[4] and then stepped out to greet the ȻȽ- EN¸Á SÁ¸ESET TŦE SḰEḰEL.[5] As SYÁ¸TEN watched the SḰEḰEL[6] rise over MEMEXÁȽ[7] and the sky change from darkness to light, she traced the distinctive shape along the back of MEMEXÁȽ, so named for the rounded back its namesake showed while inching along. SYÁ¸TEN smiled as she surveyed her environment, the beautiful view, and the ĆEḴÁU¸TW̱[8] her family had gathered to help build in the new Á¸LEṈ¸ENEȻ[9] they had started. It had been a difficult year, but here they were.

On her journey, SYÁ¸TEN walked for a very long time. In her travels she walked past a great many places of significance for the W̱SÁNEĆ Peoples before eventually coming to rest next to STOTEL¸EU.[10] While SYÁ¸TEN was resting, she heard the sound of birds and realized she

1 Journey
2 Widow
3 Baby
4 to make fire
5 Rising Sun
6 Sun
7 Caterpillar
8 Longhouse
9 Village
10 Creek

could smell T̲ŁÁŁSE[11]—and she knew she was near the sea. As she made her way toward the ocean sounds, she suddenly walked into an area surrounded by maple trees. Beautiful tall leafy ȾŦÁ,EŁĆ.[12] She decided then that this place was W̱JOŁEŁP—"The place of maples."

The W̱SÁNEĆ Peoples began to visit SYÁ,TEN, and they discovered the beauty of W̱JOŁEŁP. They helped SYÁ,TEN to build a shelter, to gather resources from the nearby sea, and to hunt and gather from the TEN̲EW̱—the land. Eventually a group moved permanently to W̱JOŁEŁP and a communal ĆEḴÁU,TW̱—the first W̱JOŁEŁP longhouse—was built. It was here that SYÁ,TEN gave birth to QOMQEM WÍ,ḴE, a strong baby boy.

That is the story of W̱JOŁEŁP.

SYÁ,TEN heard the stirring from inside the ĆEḴÁU,TW̱ as her ḴAḴ began to wake. She smiled to herself and grabbed some fresh firewood before heading inside.

HÍSW̱ḴE SIAM

11 Saltwater
12 Maple

A W̱SÁNEĆ PARADIGM

We used to live several families in one longhouse, but the government decided they didn't like that. One day they came onto the reserve and burned down all our longhouses. At the time our great-grandmother's house was overgrown with blackberry bushes and so they couldn't see it, so they missed it. It became a gathering place for the W̱SÁNEĆ people.

—Lola Garcia, personal communication, December 2015

In [Edna Manitowabi's] retelling of [the Great Flood], she asks us to think of ourselves as Zhaashkoonh, the muskrat. This emphasizes the idea that we each have to dive down to the bottom of the vast expanse of water and search for our own handful of earth. Each of us having to struggle and sacrifice to achieve re-creation is not an easy process. We each need to bring that earth to the surface, to our community, with the intent of transformation.

—Leanne Betasamosake Simpson, *Dancing On Our Turtle's Back*, 2011

> The cohabitation of Western science and Indigenous knowledge on campuses has the power of opening a dialogue among cultures and enhancing our shared knowledge.
>
> —Universities Canada "principles on Indigenous education," 2015

The W̱SÁNEĆ Nation is located at the southern end of Vancouver Island. As noted earlier, a large part of our traditional lands has been renamed the "Saanich Peninsula"—a phonetic spelling of our traditional W̱SÁNEĆ name. Prior to colonization, W̱SÁNEĆ Knowledge transfer involved embodied knowledge and experiential learning. Engaging in W̱SÁNEĆ ways of being (ontology), ways of knowing (epistemology), and ways of doing (axiology and methodology), was not possible without those embodied and experiental components. In traditional pre-contact W̱SÁNEĆ living several generations of W̱SÁNEĆ families lived in one longhouse or bighouse, and this was a key component of fostering community and enhancing W̱SÁNEĆ Knowledge transfer. In *Saltwater People,* Dave Elliott Sr. states:

> Those people were the teachers. From the time of understanding when a child began to think, the teaching had already started. Your mother, father, your uncles, your aunts, your older brothers, sisters, your grandparents were all your teachers.[13]

Residential schools and Indian day schools were effective in disrupting this process and were key in the destabilization of traditional W̱SÁNEĆ Knowledge transfer. Instead, W̱SÁNEĆ children were forced to sit in colonial classroom settings and learn to think from the neck up. They experienced disembodied teaching and learning.

13 Dave Elliott Sr., *Saltwater People*, School District No. 63, Saanich, BC (1983), 79.

W̱SÁNEĆ KNOWLEDGE AND COLONIZATION

Western education has always been of great importance for the W̱SÁNEĆ Nation. Each of the four W̱SÁNEĆ reserve areas (W̱JOȽEȽP [Tsartlip], SȾÁUTW̱ [Tsawout], BOḰEĆEN [Pauquachin], and W̱SIḴEṀ [Tseycum]) has a separate government-imposed Chief and Council governing system. Each Chief and Council has one council member assigned to the education portfolio. The education council member is responsible for meeting with the surrounding non-Indigenous school districts to facilitate dialogue, with the goal of improving the educational experiences of W̱SÁNEĆ youth. Additionally, the education council member is responsible for attending interviews and board meetings for ȽÁU, WELṈEW̱, our tribal school, which is located within W̱SÁNEĆ territory. ȽÁU, WELṈEW̱ is the product of decades of struggle and effort led primarily by W̱SÁNEĆ women. I learned of the history and development of the W̱SÁNEĆ education system through written transcripts provided to me by W̱SÁNEĆ community member Denise Sam. The transcripts were part of interviews Denise had conducted for a school project in 2016. The interviewees had participated in various capacities toward the development of the W̱SÁNEĆ education system. They included Marie Cooper, Freda Cooper, Remi Paul, Joanne Claxton, and Glenn Jim.[14]

Per the interviewees, prior to the development of what is now called the Saanich Indian School Board (SISB), W̱SÁNEĆ children were taken from our nation to attend residential schools located further up Vancouver Island or on the mainland. Alternately, they attended the day school located on the present site of the SISB. In the earliest days, which were, according to interviewees' memories, the 1950s and '60s, W̱SÁNEĆ women attended the Tsartlip Indian Day School as volunteers to aid with their children's care. This was so the women could maintain a W̱SÁNEĆ connection

14 Personal communication, Elder interviews, 2016.

for the children while also monitoring the teaching practices of the nuns who ran the school. After the 1969 White Paper written by the Pierre Trudeau government and the 1970 Red Paper response from Harold Cardinal and the Indian Association of Alberta, the government began closing both the residential and the day schools.[15] The W̱SÁNEĆ women took this opportunity to begin advocating for more involvement in the educational process of their children. They had legitimate concerns about the fate of W̱SÁNEĆ children should the Tsartlip day school close and W̱SÁNEĆ children suddenly integrated into and forced to attend non-Indigenous schools.[16]

Prior to the 1970s, the W̱SÁNEĆ women had already begun to organize. In addition to voluntarily attending the school to work as unpaid teaching assistants, they were also organizing outside of the classrooms. Early on they attempted to become part of the Parent-Teacher Association (PTA) but the $300.00 cost of establishing a new PTA chapter was far beyond their economic means. As an alternative, the W̱SÁNEĆ women became members of the BC Homemakers' Society. Once they had an established group name, and with the help of a priest named Father Mudge, they eventually applied for and received funding to buy school buses for the W̱SÁNEĆ Nation. They organized the purchase of one large bus and two smaller buses, affectionately remembered as the "bunny buses." W̱SÁNEĆ women drove the buses on a voluntary basis, with the bunny buses driving kids to local nursery and kindergartens and the larger bus driving the older kids to Tsartlip School. Even back then, the W̱SÁNEĆ women knew the importance of introducing the younger children to the dominant culture in order to avoid a culture shock later in life. After the 1970 Red Paper, the W̱SÁNEĆ women began organizing to take control of W̱SÁNEĆ education.[17]

15 Indian Association of Alberta, *Citizens Plus* (Red Paper), prepared by Harold Cardinal, 1970. https://www.thecanadianencyclopedia.ca/en/article/citizens-plus-the-red-paper

16 Personal communication, Elder interviews, 2016.

17 Personal communication, Elder interviews, 2016.

Once the W̱SÁNEĆ women saw that the federal government intended to permanently close the Tsartlip day school, they began to forcefully request that the school remain open. With the help of Father Mudge, they incorporated their group and became the Saanich Indian School Board, after which they were able to apply for federal funding. It is because of this small group of volunteer women that the present W̱SÁNEĆ education system exists. W̱SÁNEĆ now has a nursery, kindergarten, junior high, high school, and the Saanich Adult Education Centre (SAEC). The SAEC is the entity responsible for the distribution and maintenance of the funding for post-secondary students. The SAEC also functions as a satellite school, working with Camosun College for upgrading, college preparatory courses, and special diploma programs. I have been a grateful recipient of the SAEC funding, and have had the pleasure of working with the eternally patient and supportive staff. It is inspiring to realize this all began with a group of W̱SÁNEĆ women concerned about the future of education for W̱SÁNEĆ children.[18]

A concern W̱SÁNEĆ community members realized early on, and that continues to be at the fore of education plans today, is the issue of finding a balance between traditional W̱SÁNEĆ education (cultural practices and language, etc.) and eurocentric westernized pedagogy. W̱SÁNEĆ community members advocate more for one or the other depending on whether they are concerned with adherence to W̱SÁNEĆ traditional lands and practices or with how their children will fare in dominant society once they leave W̱SÁNEĆ schools. Traditional W̱SÁNEĆ Knowledge is embodied through experiential practices, and contemporary W̱SÁNEĆ learners face challenges our ancestors did not. In my own journey through postsecondary education, as I progressed through college, undergraduate, and then graduate studies, I noticed and experienced an increased pressure to conform and submit to dominant

18 Personal communication, Elder interviews, 2016.

eurocentric pedagogy. The would become central issue that would ultimately cause me to leave the Trent University campus, the city of Peterborough, and the province of Ontario.

TOL, NEW̱ SEN TŦE SOȽ

In 2014, I began the journey toward a doctorate from Trent University, and the two-and-a-half years I spent on campus were traumatic and life-altering. After that time, I had no choice but to leave. My journey toward a doctorate began with trauma before progressing through a course full of obstacles, conflicts, and challenges. I now find myself in a place of strength, and having survived the harrowing journey, I've come out changed on the other side. I am safe, I am loved, I am healing, I am growing, and I am in recovery. There were forces on the Trent University campus that I inevitably came into conflict with, in large part because I refused to allow non-Indigenous pedagogy to dictate how I conducted and wrote W̱SÁNEĆ research. Due to this refusal, I was subjected to tactics and pressures that very nearly broke me—and very nearly succeeded in making me quit. But I am still here, and I am still writing. TOL, NEW̱ SEN TŦE SOȽ—I know the road.

Indigenous people who stand up for themselves and speak their minds are often labelled as "difficult" or "unprofessional" by those in power. In my education journey, I have often heard Indigenous scholars that I admire described as "angry" by my seminar cohorts. For example, Eve Tuck and Wayne Yang, authors of *Decolonization is Not a Metaphor*, and Sheila Cote-Meek, author of *Colonized Classrooms*, are a few of the scholars that I have heard described in this way for simply articulating the truth. Neither of these works are angry enough, in my opinion, and do not even scratch the surface when it comes to the trauma inflicted upon Indigenous scholars in the academy. When Indigenous students enter these ivory towers, the expectation is for them to conform to the academy. The expectation is for Indigenous students to do all the work of reconciling a very specific kind of Indigenous Knowledge with the academy. It must be filtered and shaped to fit pre-existing molds, and there are very strict rules put in place to make sure that that happens.

When I left the Trent University campus, I left Ontario and moved back to the W̱SÁNEĆ Nation, in part because I had finished the required coursework and my research was better served by relocating closer to the W̱SÁNEĆ Nation. Unfortunately, the other part was because I could no longer stay in a situation that I found hostile and oppressive. After I returned to the safe environment of W̱SÁNEĆ territories, I was able to resume my dissertation research. As a reaction to my experiences at Trent University and as a natural extension to my dissertation, I developed an interest in questions of how and why academia is set up the way that it is. I wanted to know why there was such pressure for me to research W̱SÁNEĆ Knowledge in such a specific and rigid manner, and why I was met with such disdain for choosing to focus instead on W̱SÁNEĆ/Indigenous paradigms. To understand, I knew I would have to find the scholars out there who were writing about alternatives to social science rhetoric. I discovered prolific and inspirational scholars unafraid to speak up and take on the status quo.

IGNORANCE AND THE UNIVERSITY EXPERIENCE

> For what is most of our boasted so-called knowledge but a conceit that we know something, which robs us of the advantage of our actual ignorance? What we call knowledge is often our positive ignorance, ignorance our negative knowledge.
>
> —Henry David Thoreau, *Walking,* 1851

I begin with this quote because it became vital to the next stage in my dissertation research. I had come to a place in my academic journey where I was questioning why I was there. I could not in good conscience ignore who I was and simply cave to the demands that

I conform to the institution and engage with W̱SÁNEĆ Knowledge by filtering it through non-Indigenous theory and methodologies. I was informed that it was not possible to utilize an Indigenous paradigm, because such a thing did not exist, and to create one was deemed out of the question. Why? I could not understand how the choices in my research could even affect those detractors in any way, shape, or form; they didn't, and yet these detractors still felt the need to deter me—which brings me to a second quote from Thoreau:

> A man's ignorance sometimes is not only useful but beautiful—while his knowledge, so called, is oftentimes worse than useless, beside being ugly. Which is the best man to deal with: He who knows nothing about a subject, and, what is extremely rare, knows that he knows nothing, or he who really knows something about it but thinks that he knows all?[19]

The Indigenous Studies PhD Program included a second-year course called "Dissertation Research Course." The Trent University Indigenous Studies Ph.D. Program Student Handbook offered the following course description:

> INDG 6701 is designed to support students in developing an appropriate plan to carry out research for their dissertation. Students work through the various stages of proposal development. At this time, students begin working with their Dissertation Supervisor and Supervisory Committee to complete a proposal that can be defended trough the dissertation proposal defence examination process.[20]

19 Henry David Thoreau, *Walden and Selected Essays* (New York : Hendricks House, 1951).
20 Trent University Indigenous Studies Ph.D. Program Student Handbook, 2014, 33.

The seminar course was scheduled to meet once a month during the second term of our second year. We received an email about a month prior to the first seminar, in which we were instructed to forward a copy of our dissertation proposals (or what we had at that time) to our cohort and the two seminar instructors. We were also asked to prepare dissertation proposal presentations. The email stated that we would be allowed twenty minutes for a presentation, followed by ten to fifteen minutes of questions. There were only two of us in the cohort at that time. Also present were one professor and an Indigenous Studies instructor who holds a Masters of Business Administration.

I highlight this experience because it was a pivotal moment for me. At that time, I was questioning the structure of Indigenous Studies PhD program at Trent University as well as my continued pursuit of a doctorate altogether. I was wary of this seminar course because I had learned that the program expected research to be conducted through a social science research framework. I knew what the program leaders wanted, and I knew that I had no intention of doing it. I had already done a very deep dive into Indigenous scholars who were working against non-Indigenous theory and methodologies. I knew that scholars such as Margaret Kovach and Jo-Anne Archibald had authored entire books in which they shared their early research experiences of attempting to use such theory and methodologies. According to these scholars, it was not until they focused on Indigenous research theory and methodologies that their research began to make sense for them. The dissertation proposal I presented was approximately eighteen pages in length, and what I ultimately successfully defended was twenty-eight pages in length. The content did not change except insofar as I expanded upon the earlier dissertation proposal format and written components.

I knew that I had a good dissertation proposal and a solid understanding of the how and why of my research. Because I was researching the W̱SÁNEĆ Nation, and because my work was about me and my people, it was very straightforward to me. I had been working on this research for years up to this point, and was well prepared. I did the introduction in the SENĆOŦEN language, but when I put up the first slide, I barely got a few sentences in before I was interrupted with a question. There were no "twenty minutes and then questions" for me. I spent the next forty-five minutes defending my research and dissertation proposal slide by slide against the two instructors. I am proud that I remained calm and answered every question thrown at me. I even asked a few questions of my own and I defended my work. By the time I reached the last slide, I was exhausted and angry. This was our very first meeting for this seminar and the first opportunity for the cohort to present our dissertation proposals. It had been my understanding that it was a presentation followed by questions, instead what I received felt like an attack on everything about my research. What had happened to the course "designed to support students in developing an appropriate plan to carry out research for their dissertation," as stated in the course description? Constructive criticism and scholarly guidance were nowhere to be found.

As I write this, there is an interesting document making the rounds on social media. It is one of those recurring posts because of its relevance to the turbulent times we live in. The *Simple Sabotage Field Manual: Strategic Services* (1944) was published by the Office of Strategic Services in Washington D.C. (the OSS was the precursor to the CIA).[21] It is resurfacing on social media now because of the section pertaining to the disruption and sabotage of organizations and conferences (or any other event of which sabotage is desired). I obviously cannot say that the two instructors engaged in deliberate sabotage during my dissertation proposal presentation, because that is simply outlandish and feels too petty to consider. However, I will admit that a few of the OSS suggestions were familiar enough that they made me laugh. The following snippets are taken from page twenty-eight of the document:

21 Office of Strategic Services, *The Simple Sabotage Field Manual (Provisional)* (Washington, D.C, 1944).

1. "Talk as frequently as possible and at great length."

   I was interrupted as soon as I started my presentation, and this continued throughout a full forty-five minutes. I never had the opportunity to do a presentation from start to finish. I fielded questions instead.

2. "Bring up irrelevant issues."

   They did this by asking questions that were not directly related to my research. They also repeatedly veered off topic to discuss points that I would have arrived at later in the presentation if I had been allowed to actually present. Twice I had to say, "if you would just let me continue with the presentation, that question will be answered in an upcoming slide."

3. "Haggle over precise wordings."

   This was done over and over. I recall that my interlocutors wanted to haggle over whether it was "Embodied Indigenous Knowledge" or "Indigenous Embodied Knowledge," and honestly, it did not matter. At another point, one of them was insistent that all seminars are embodied and therefore weren't we embodying a seminar at that moment?

It was frustrating because I knew they were being willfully obtuse about my research, so that even if they were not engaging in deliberate sabotage, they were at least being obstructive. This is also covered in the OSS document, under the heading "General Devices for Lowering Morale and Creating Confusion," which simply states: "Act stupid."[22]

This was the one and only time we met for this seminar. It was such an obvious disaster and so completely unhelpful for everyone involved that we never had to do it again. The class was meant to

22 Office of Strategic Services, *The Simple Sabotage Field Manual*," 31.

nurture and guide our research, but instead it was used to waste time with silly games. When I consider the situation in light of the Thoreau quotes at the beginning of this section, it was not so much that we were coming from different epistemological perspectives; it was more that the instructors were showing the reality of their pedagogy. Their knowledge was nothing more than "a conceit that [they] know something," and while their "knowledge, so called, is oftentimes worse than useless, beside being ugly," I had no desire to engage with an obviously conceited and ugly knowledge.

CENTERING INDIGENOUS KNOWLEDGES

I have since made it my mission to include in my practice, alternatives to the way that PhD research is typically done. I have since discovered *Research as Resistance*, edited by Leslie Brown and Susan Strega, and *The Authentic Dissertation: Alternative Ways of Knowing, Research, and Representation*, edited by Four Arrows (Don Trent Jacobs). In *Research as Resistance* the editors state, "One of these common themes [in the edited collection] is a willingness to explore the emancipatory possibilities of new approaches to research, even when these transgress the boundaries of traditional research and scholarship."[23] In *The Authentic Dissertation*, editor Four Arrows has compiled award-winning and unique PhD dissertations that offer alternatives to standard dissertation formats.[24] Both books inspired me to look beyond what the Trent program was demanding in a dissertation. They showed me that there were far more options out there than the cookie-cutter social science format. Beyond the invitation they offered to push the envelope in terms of form, these books challenged me to examine more closely the *why* of what the university was asking of me. So, I kept researching.

23 Leslie Brown and Susan Strega, eds., *Research as Resistance: Critical, Indigenous, and Anti-oppressive Approaches* (Toronto: Canadian Scholar's Press, 2005), 1.

24 Four Arrows (Don Trent Jacobs), ed., *The Authentic Dissertation: Alternative Ways of Knowing, Research, and Representation* (London & New York: Taylor & Francis, 2008).

The previous quotes from Thoreau can be found in *Epistemologies of Ignorance in Education*, edited by Erik Malewski and Nathalia Jaramillo. This book was my first glimpse into an alternative to social science pedagogy, and I was entranced. I thoroughly enjoyed the thought that expertise in one area meant ignorance in another because we simply cannot know everything. Erik Malewski sums it up perfectly:

> The scholarship that makes up this collection, then, becomes a middle way, a sort of "one foot in one foot out" of the positivity of knowledge, reading with and against disciplinarity, emphasizing ambivalence alongside certainty, unknowing alongside knowledge, and breakdowns alongside continuities.[25]

The book covers multiple disciplines and perspectives while it examines the question of knowing and unknowing in education. It was an introduction to alternative ways of knowing in opposition to what was presented to me at Trent, but the main benefit of the collection was that it introduced me to the work of Walter D. Mignolo. Mignolo's research focuses on different aspects of the modern and colonial world, exploring concepts such as global coloniality, the geopolitics of knowledge, transmodernity, and border thinking.

During that problematic dissertation proposal presentation, while I was defending myself and my research, I was also questioning the questioners about why I was expected to conduct research in the way that they wanted. Why was I expected to use theories and methodologies I already knew were not suitable? I knew that the countless articles and books that I had read by Indigenous scholars did not really take off until they left behind ideas of fitting Indigenous Knowledge into eurocentric western paradigms. The consensus was that it was like trying to fit a square peg into a round hole—it just did not work. One of the questions I posed therefore

25 Erik Malewski and Nathalia Jaramillo, eds., *Epistemologies of Ignorance in Education* (Charlotte, NC: Information Age Publishing, 2011), 4.

was: why we were still expected to repeat this process when it had been attempted multiple times without success? I pointed out the common notion that the definition of insanity was doing the same thing over and over and expecting different results. I wanted to know why good research could not simply be. Why could it not stand alone, but instead had to be circumscribed by such specific research frameworks? I had questions, but no answers were forthcoming at that time.

My cohort was fortunate to have Leanne Betasamosake Simpson as a guest lecturer in a few seminars. In one seminar, she shared the story of how she never intended for *Dancing on Our Turtle's Back* to be an academic book. Simpson authored the book for the Anishinaabeg people, and she was very clear that it was never intended for the academy. I pointed out during the dissertation proposal presentation that this book did not produce Indigenous Knowledge through the dominant paradigms, and absolutely did not follow the format that was at that time being forced upon me. Yet it had been assigned as required reading in almost every single Indigenous Studies PhD seminar at Trent University. I wanted to know why I could not write a dissertation about W̱SÁNEĆ Knowledge in the same vein. There were no responses to any of my questions or statements that day.

There are several aspects of Walter D. Mignolo's "Epistemic Disobedience, Independent Thought and De-Colonial Freedom" that were pure revelations for me. One short description is worth quoting in full:

> Briefly, the formal apparatus of enunciation is the basic apparatus for engaging in institutional and purposive knowledge-making geo-politically oriented. Originally theology was the overarching conceptual and cosmological frame of knowledge-making in which social actors engaged and institutions (monasteries, churches, universities, states, etc.) were created. Secularization,

> in the 18th century, displaced Christian theology and secular philosophy and science took its place.[26]

Institutional knowledge-making required that an agreed-upon language be developed so that the enunciators could discuss amongst themselves the enunciated. Mignolo writes: "While in everyday life frames are not regulated but rather operate through consensual agreements, disciplinary knowledge requires more complex and regulated frames known today as 'scholarly disciplines'."[27] He also notes that "[t]he history of knowledge-making in modern Western history from the Renaissance on will have, then, theology and philosophy-science as the two cosmological frames," and that "[b]oth frames are institutionally and linguistically anchored in Western Europe."[28] We see then that the development of institutional knowledge-making was a very eurocentric western project from its inception.

How are Indigenous Knowledges perceived and located in these "cosmological frames"? They are not. Mignolo discusses his elaboration

> on enunciation and knowledge-making focusing on the borders between the Western (in the precise linguistic and institutional sense [that he defines]) foundation of knowledge and understanding (epistemology and hermeneutics) and its confrontation with knowledge-making in non-European languages and institutions in China, in the Islamic Caliphate, or education in the institutions of the Maya, Aztecs and Incas that the Encyclopaedia Britannica has deigned

26 Walter Mignolo, "Epistemic Disobedience, Independent Thought and De-colonial Freedom, *Theory, Culture & Society* 26 (2009), 18.

27 Mignolo, "Epistemic Disobedience, Independent Thought and De-colonial Freedom," 6.

28 Mignolo, "Epistemic Disobedience, Independent Thought and De-colonial Freedom," 6.

> to describe as "education in primitive and early civilizations."[29]

It is clear then, that Indigenous Knowledges would be categorized as "education in primitive and early civilizations," and therefore would not be included in the previous knowledge-making cosmological frames founded by and within western institutions. Indigenous Knowledge has always been outside of the university system.

As non-western and non-eurocentric, Indigenous Peoples were and are considered inferior in many ways. Mignolo facetiously states:

> Places of nonthought (of myth, non-western religions, folklore, underdevelopment involving regions and people) today have been waking up from the long process of westernization. The anthropos inhabiting non-European places discovered that s/he had been invented, as anthropos, by a locus of enunciations self-defined as humanitas.[30]

This *self-definition* is extremely important, as it calls to mind the sleight of hand in the creation of past and present intellectual hierarchies. Who exactly created them and why? On this point, Mignolo writes, "In the three worlds of distribution of scientific labor, the First World had indeed the *privilege of inventing the classification and being part of it.*"[31] Finally, I was beginning to find answers to the questions I had posed during my dissertation proposal presentation.

Walter D. Mignolo was the scholar I had been searching for, and in his writing, I began to find the answers I had been seeking.

29 Mignolo, "Epistemic Disobedience, Independent Thought and De-colonial Freedom," 7.

30 Mignolo, "Epistemic Disobedience, Independent Thought and De-colonial Freedom," 3.

31 Mignolo, "Epistemic Disobedience, Independent Thought and De-colonial Freedom," 8. Italics in original.

Within the PhD program at Trent, I felt such powerlessness. I experienced so much oppression and when I questioned that oppression, I was greeted with silence. In his work, Mignolo is very clear "that it is not enough to change the content of the conversation, that it is of the essence to change the terms of the conversation," and that "[a]s far as controversies and interpretations remain within the same rules of the game (terms of the conversation), the control of knowledge is not called into question."[32] According to Mignolo, we need to stop playing by their rules and start asking why they are so desperate for us to work the way they want us to. We need to change the conversation from defensive to offensive.

The game has always been rigged in the institution's favour, and any opposition is easily met and overcome because the institution is set up as the judge and jury. This has been well hidden because according to Mignolo:

> The basic assumption is that the knower is always implicated, geo- and body-politically, in the known, although modern epistemology (e.g. the hubris of the zero point) managed to conceal both and created the figure of the detached observer, a neutral seeker of truth and objectivity who at the same time controls the disciplinary rules and puts himself or herself in a privileged position to evaluate and dictate.[33]

"Epistemic Disobedience, Independent Thought, and De-Colonial Freedom" was revolutionary for my research—and for my outlook on graduate studies and the university system. Mignolo's work provided the answers to why university knowledge-making was structured the way it was and gave me assurances that the power dynamic I'd experienced while at Trent University was in fact real.

32 Mignolo, "Epistemic Disobedience, Independent Thought and De-colonial Freedom," 4.

33 Mignolo, "Epistemic Disobedience, Independent Thought and De-colonial Freedom," 4.

However, different questions questions I'd posed, about why we were expected to engage through social science in such a narrow and specific manner, would be answered in a different article that Mignolo published in 2014.

One of the issues I found confusing about the program at Trent was the aggressiveness of the social science rhetoric. The two white professors and the MBA-holder each made a point of telling me "*We* are social sciences, and *you* are humanities" as if this somehow excused or was an adequate explanation for the unfair treatment I received for drafting a dissertation proposal from a W̱SÁNEĆ Knowledge perspective. I majored in political science for a BA from the University of Victoria (social sciences), and my MA was from York University's Theatre and Performance Studies program (humanities). However, I was in an Indigenous Studies PhD program that I considered to be neither social sciences nor humanities. There was something angry and oppressive about the insistence from these individuals that I write from a social sciences perspective, followed by an unnecessary categorization and dismissal once it became clear I had no intention of following those orders. I am an Indigenous Studies scholar researching W̱SÁNEĆ Knowledges, and social sciences/humanities are in no way a part of that—period.

In Walter D. Mignolo's "Spirit Out of Bounds Returns to the East: The Closing of the Social Sciences and the Opening of Independent Thoughts," he refers to "The Gulbenkian Report."[34] The 1996 article "Open the Social Sciences" was based on a talk Immanuel Wallerstein gave to the Social Science Research Council in 1995. Wallerstein was the chair of the Gulbenkian Commission when they met three times during the years 1994 and 1995. What stood out to me on reading this article was the conceit of the social

34 Walter D. Mignolo, "Spirit out of Bounds Returns to the East: The Closing of the Social Sciences and the Opening of Independent Thoughts," *Current Sociology* 62,4 (June 2014): 584-602; Immanuel Wallerstein, *Open the Social Sciences: Report of the Gulbenkian Commission on the Restructuring of the Social Sciences* (Stanford: Stanford University Press, 1996).

scientists involved in the Gulbenkian Commission. They had absolute certainty that they held the key to the next stage of social science restructuring and a complete lack of awareness that perhaps many did not share their vision. Some of us would prefer not to restructure the social sciences, but instead to find alternative research theories and methodologies.

At one point in the article, Wallerstein laments "the tripartite division itself—humanities, social science, natural science—is coming into question."[35] Wallerstein is wary of the intermingling and blurring of the disciplines, and this wariness is reminiscent of the way the two white professors and the MBA-holder categorized the humanities and social sciences in their effort to distance themselves from me and my research. In an earlier section of the article Wallerstein criticized the proliferation of alternative knowledges such as those in women's studies and Black studies (to which, I surmise, he would add Indigenous studies). Wallerstein's main question, then is how to restructure, or how to "try to rethink new rationales, new ways of divisioning," with the goal of reshaping the social sciences and fixing it so that it remained under a social sciences framework, and control.[36] It is from this perspective that Mignolo's 2014 article commences.

Mignolo states that "[t]he social sciences expanded around the world. They became the empire companion. Like in any other sphere of imperial expansion, those who are happy with the expansion are those enacting it" and "[t]hose who have to endure the consequences may adapt and surrender, or delink."[37] It goes without saying then, that the above-described academics in the Indigenous Studies PhD program at Trent University would qualify as both "those who are happy with" and "those enacting" the social sciences' continued cognitive imperialism. Indigenous scholars, intellectuals, and activists have been challenging this cognitive imperialism for decades now. Given the choice, I too choose to delink.

35 Wallerstein, *Open the Social Sciences*, 6.
36 Wallerstein, *Open the Social Sciences*, 6.
37 Mignolo, "Spirit out of Bounds Returns to the East," 585.

As though responding to my previous question regarding why good research cannot just be, without the forced social sciences format, Mignolo writes that "[p]eople around the world have been and continue to be good thinkers without recourse to the 'social sciences,'" and that "[b]eyond the reasons Western social scientists may have to defend and promote the social sciences, they are not the only options."[38] It is good to question the programs, professors, and institutions responsible for knowledge-making rather than to passively submit to indoctrination. Mignolo further elaborates:

> It would be pretentious and arrogant if Western social scientists appointed themselves to solve the problems that European imperialism created in other latitudes. And it would be pure submission if thinkers from other latitudes identify their problems starting from Western social sciences instead of starting from the consequences of coloniality of knowledge in their own local histories.[39]

I wanted the opportunity to write about WSÁNEC Knowledge without having to resort to filtering it through a social sciences framework before it would be deemed acceptable by certain academics at Trent.

Another thinker who has influenced how I think of scholarship, and who I encountered through Mignolo, is Boaventura de Sousa Santos. Santos was born in Portugal, and is a professor of sociology as well as a distinguished legal scholar. Santos is prolific and has published widely on globalization, sociology of law and the state, epistemology, democracy, and human rights. I was first introduced to his work through his book *The End of the Cognitive Empire*. This book is both an amalgamation of and an expansion upon his previous scholarship surrounding what he terms "the abyssal line."[40]

38 Mignolo, "Spirit out of Bounds Returns to the East," 586-587.

39 Mignolo, "Spirit out of Bounds Returns to the East," 590.

40 Boaventura de Sousa Santos, *The End of the Cognitive Empire: the Coming of Age of Epistemologies of the South* (Durham: Duke University Press, 2018), 3-16.

In Santos's work, he establishes epistemologies of the North and epistemologies of the South, and then further divides them with the abyssal line. When Santos uses North and South, he points out they are not geographically located, but instead represent an ideology that distinguishes worldviews. The abyssal line therefore is a versatile concept.

Santos provides as an example a student of colour attending an Ivy league university. On campus, they are treated no differently than any other student, and so they would be considered to be the northern side of the abyssal line. However, as soon as they leave campus and are confronted by police officers, they have crossed the abyssal line to the southern side. Similarly, Indigenous knowledges exist in the epistemologies of the South. Our knowledges are specific to our locations. For example, WSÁNEC Knowledges are very much connected to our practices on the land and sea because we are surrounded by water. Indigenous Knowledges from the prairie provinces would be completely different, since the people there have no access to the sea. Indigenous Knowledges can and have been extracted from Indigenous epistemologies of the South and reformatted to fit academia's eurocentric knowledge-making systems. The social sciences have been very good at extracting Indigenous Knowledges for their purposes and changing them to fit the university epistemologies of the North. Academia's eurocentric social science knowledge-making systems therefore form part of the epistemologies of the North, and since we know from Mignolo's scholarship that Indigenous Knowledges are considered inferior and primitive, they will forever form part of the epistemologies of the South.

Santos states, "I have been arguing that modern science, particularly modern social sciences, including critical theories, have never acknowledged the existence of the abyssal line."[41] It is beneficial for social scientists to ignore or deny the existence of an abyssal line

41 Santos, *The End of the Cognitive Empire*, 19.

because acknowledging one would mean admitting that they participate in—and have always participated in—the purposeful exclusion of non-western knowledges. Worse, they would have to acknowledge their tactics of forced knowledge assimilation. Santos writes:

> The epistemologies of the South have to proceed according to what I call the sociology of absences, that is to say, turning absent subjects into present subjects as the foremost condition for identifying and validating knowledges that may reinvent social emancipation and liberation.[42]

Liberation and emancipation from the social sciences hegemony is a commitment in the project of "epistemic disobedience" to which Mignolo refers. However, it is not a simple case of sending social scientists into Indigenous communities to extract and appropriate knowledges and then reformatting those knowledges for the university. Santos cautions against such vanguard intellectuals, and notes that "[i]nstead, the epistemologies of the South call for rearguard intellectuals, intellectuals that contribute with their knowledge to strengthening the social struggles against domination and oppression to which they are committed."[43] Therefore, the sociology of absences needs to come directly from Indigenous Knowledges and not from the social sciences' interpretation of Indigenous Knowledges.

One of the primary objectives of Santos' scholarship is found in his statement that "we don't need another theory of revolution; we need rather to revolutionize theory."[44] According to Santos, we must do this by first collectively acknowledging the abyssal line, after which we must collectively develop the appropriate post-abyssal pedagogy—a pedagogy that is more inclusive of Indigenous epistemologies of the South as they are, and not reconfigured

42 Santos, *The End of the Cognitive Empire*, 2.
43 Santos, *The End of the Cognitive Empire*, xi.
44 Santos, *The End of the Cognitive Empire*, xi.

according to social sciences rules. He further elaborates that "[s]ince colonialism is a co-creation, however asymmetrical, decolonizing entails decolonizing both the knowledge of the colonized and the knowledge of the colonizer."[45] To revolutionize theory, according to Santos, we need Indigenous scholars capable of engaging with both epistemologies of the North and epistemologies of the South, who have a solid grounding in their respective Indigenous Knowledges. Additionally, there is a need for university scholars working in epistemologies of the North willing to acknowledge and promote Indigenous scholars coming from epistemologies of the South. Santos cautions that this will be problematic because those scholars will be criticized, and their work deemed less scholarly by the Northern epistemological scholars—i.e., social scientists.

Syed Hussein Alatas was a prominent Malaysian social scientist and public intellectual. His son Syed Farid Alatas, a Malaysian national, is a Professor of Sociology at the National University of Singapore. I found the Drs. Alatas's writing to be vital for my research. I was particularly drawn to Syed Farid Alatas's argument that:

> The institutional and theoretical dependence of scholars in developing societies on Western social science has resulted in what has been referred to as the 'captive mind'. The phenomenon of the captive mind refers to a way of thinking that is dominated by Western thought in an imitative and uncritical manner. Among the characteristics of the captive mind are the inability to be creative and raise original problems, the inability to devise original analytical methods, and alienation from the main issues of indigenous society.[46]

45 Santos, *The End of the Cognitive Empire*, 107.
46 Syed Farid Alatas, "The Sacralization of the Social Sciences: a Critique of an Emerging Theme in Academic Discourse," *Archives de Sciences Sociales des Religions* 91 (July-Sept 1995), 90.

Though S. F. Alatas is referring to scholars in non-western countries here, his *captive mind* theory can easily be applied to Indigenous scholars as well. S. F. Alatas warns that "[w]hat is regarded as a problem is the uncritical imitation of the social sciences in the Third World."[47] The main difference, however, is in how those other countries import western social sciences, whereas Indigenous academics in Canada are unavoidably trained in them. Indigenous people have no choice but to leave our respective communities to attend university. Therefore, the wholesale acceptance of western social sciences and the captive mind is almost a given.

S. H. Alatas juxtaposes the captive mind and the independent mind using the following analogy:

> An Asian may adopt communism but as a communist he can be a captive mind or an independent mind. If he is independent he will adapt communist philosophy to the Asian setting, extricating what is culturally Western from the general philosophical components of communism.[48]

The goal, then, is not to become an Indigenous scholar with a captive mind who uncritically accepts the forced social science rhetoric. This is not such an easy task when one considers how most Indigenous people in Canada face obstacles to maintaining our Indigeneity. For example, many Indigenous Peoples lack the benefits of learning our languages from birth because of language loss in Indigenous communities. Another major issue is how currently fifty percent of Indigenous Peoples are located outside of their traditional territories and grow up in urban centres. Indigenous Peoples may or may not have the benefit of participating in our social, spiritual, and cultural practices, and even if we do have access, much of the time those practices have been significantly altered by colonialism.

47 Alatas, "The Sacralization of the Social Sciences," 90.

48 Syed Hussein Alatas, "The captive mind and creative development," *International Social Science Journal* 26, 4 (1974), 692.

Should we make it as far as attending university, maintaining an Indigenous identity while attending one of colonialism's greatest producers of colonial knowledge and captive minds is extremely challenging.

S. H. Alatas then shares a story of reading a research paper to one of his classes, substituting the word "India" with the word "Singapore," and having none of the students notice. Alatas cautions that if one's scholarship is so generic that its details can be swapped out so easily, it has no point. This would be akin to me writing my dissertation about the W̱SÁNEĆ Nation and producing work so generic that no one would notice or care if I switched out the word "W̱SÁNEĆ" for "Sḵwx̱wú7mesh Úxwumixw" (Squamish). Indigenous scholarship must come from an independent mind and reflect the connection one has to one's Indigenous ancestors.

Here, S. F. Alatas refers to Third World scholarship; however, these words are useful when considering Indigenous scholars as well:

> While there is a significant amount of empirical work generated in the Third World much of this takes its cues from research in the West in terms of research agenda, theoretical perspectives and methods. This is the most important dimension of academic dependency.[49]

S. F. Alatas is advocating for a move away from academic dependency and toward Mignolo's "epistemic disobedience." While I agree that this is one of the most important dimensions of academic dependency, I believe that what S.H. Alatas terms "the recruiting agents of captivity" are equally important.[50] There are myriad ways the recruiting agents of captivity have of coercing or forcing an independent mind to become a captive one. Examples

49 Syed Farid Alatas, "Academic Dependency and the Global Division of Labour in the Social Sciences," *Current Sociology* 51, 6 (November, 2003), 604.

50 Syed Hussein Alatas, "The captive mind and creative development," 697.

such as tenure, grants, scholarships, grades, shaming, silencing, expulsion, and banishment are just a few. Those who would be considered agents of captivity have the power to assess, approve, deny, or recommend Indigenous scholars at their discretion. The question then becomes whether they show a preference for an independent thinker, or if they prefer an Indigenous scholar who has a captive mind instead.

Walter D. Mignolo, Boaventura de Sousa Santos, Syed Farid Alatas, and Syed Hussein Alatas have been publishing since the 1970s, '80s, and '90s. None of them advocate for a wholesale refusal of the dominant eurocentric western theories and methodologies, and neither does my work. Instead, what each of them advocates for are "alternative models, methodologies and concepts to modify, supplement, or substitute those already available."[51] According to these scholars, the way to accomplish this is not by filtering Indigenous Knowledges through the social sciences, but instead by beginning with our respective Indigenous Knowledges and modifying, supplementing, or substituting them as needed.

Finally, Mignolo writes that "[n]on-Western ways of knowing mean that there are other questions, genealogies of thoughts, experiences and feelings, issues that cannot be confronted by expanding the social sciences to the non-Western world," and that "[t]hus, de-westernizing and decolonizing knowledge (and knowing) means to delink from the belief that there is one way of knowing and therefore of being."[52] The continuation of the cognitive imperialism of the social sciences in Indigenous research is the preeminent question facing Indigenous researchers in the academy. The answer lies in how we as Indigenous scholars conduct our research, and ultimately in how the institutions and those in power accept or reject that research. Indigenous ontology and epistemology, or

51 Syed Hussein Alatas, "The Captive mind in development studies: Some neglected problems and the need for an autonomous social science tradition in Asia," *International Social Science Journal* XXIV, 1 (1972), 20.

52 Mignolo, "Spirit Out of Bounds Returns to the East," 595.

Indigenous ways of being and knowing, are irrevocably grounded in our lands, our traditions, our practices, and the teachings of our ancestors. For our knowledges to be ethically and accurately researched from an Indigenous perspective (paradigm), that is where they must begin. Indigenous scholars need to be allowed to engage with Indigenous research by utilizing *Indigenous* paradigms. What better way to accomplish this monumental task of delinking and paradigm-building than through the work of the brilliant and insightful Shawn Wilson?

AN INDIGENOUS AND/OR W̱SÁNEĆ PARADIGM

Shawn Wilson's *Research is Ceremony* served as a blueprint for the development and implementation of my Indigenous/W̱SÁNEĆ paradigm. The book grew from Wilson's doctoral research and, along with Leanne Betasamosake Simpson's *Dancing on Our Turtle's Back*, represents what I consider to be the epitome of good, authentic Indigenous writing. In Wilson's book, he states that he will not be comparing Indigenous paradigm components to non-Indigenous counterparts for validation, because this would only centre non-Indigenous work. He says the same thing about non-Indigenous theory and methodologies, because the goal is to establish an Indigenous paradigm and not to centre non-Indigenous scholarship.

Enroute to articulating an Indigenous paradigm, Wilson first lays out the progression of Indigenous research from contact up to the present. He passes through the now familiar phases of being discovered, written about, writing like them, writing for ourselves, finding our own voices, and now establishing our own research paradigms. This is an oversimplification of Wilson's text; however, this rough sketch leads into some of Wilson's more relevant concepts. The entire book can be read like a circle, beginning and ending with the concept of what makes an Indigenous paradigm. Within the text, Wilson employs various written voices to illustrate aspects of Indigenous pedagogy. For example, he writes to his two sons directly in an effort to establish a rapport with the reader. He also introduces his research participants in a traditional Indigenous introductory format, in addition to using personal names to honour their contributions to his research. Finally, Wilson compiles several separate interviews into one single interview to reflect a *talking circle* format for the reader. These approaches are what Wilson would term "strategies of Inquiry," described as "build[ing] upon a methodology to fill in how you will arrive at the research destination."[53] Since the research destination for Wilson is an Indigenous paradigm, these tools are necessary for the articulation.

Before Wilson can begin to unpack the particulars of an Indigenous paradigm, he first explains that:

> A paradigm is a set of underlying beliefs that guide our actions. So a research paradigm is the beliefs that guide our actions as researchers. These beliefs include the way that we view reality (ontology), how we think about or know this reality (epistemology), our ethics and morals (axiology) and how we go about gaining more knowledge about reality (methodology).[54]

Wilson cites the extensive and thorough work of Yvonna S. Lincoln and Egon G. Guba when writing about dominant paradigms. Rather than butcher his succinct two-page description of positivism, post-positivism, critical theory, and constructivism, I would instead direct you to pages 35–37 of *Research is Ceremony.* While my desire is to avoid centring non-Indigenous writing, I found myself unable to avoid Lincoln and Guba's 1994 article, which is cited in Wilson's book, as well as a response by John Heron and Peter Reason to the article, and a further response from Lincoln and Guba to Heron and Reason.

53 Wilson, *Research is Ceremony,* 39.
54 Wilson, *Research is Ceremony*, 13.

In "Competing Paradigms in Qualitative Research," Guba and Lincoln define a paradigm "as the basic belief system or worldview that guides the investigator, not only in choices of method but in ontologically and epistemologically fundamental ways."[55] Again, rather than deconstruct Guba and Lincoln's writing, I would you to the aforementioned pages of Shawn Wilson's *Research is Ceremony*. An interesting critique of this article will be explored in the Heron and Reason article that I will discuss next. However, for now I am more interested in pulling at the threads holding together these belief systems or worldviews. Guba and Lincoln disclose a preference for constructivism, and I find this important to note because of their classification of critical theory. They describe critical theory as "a blanket term denoting a set of several alternative paradigms, including additionally (but not limited to) neo-Marxism, feminism, materialism, and participatory inquiry."[56] Guba and Lincoln admit that this is a judgement call, which is in part due to their disinterest in engaging with the many different points of view embedded within the larger critical theory category.

They further articulate how "[a] paradigm may be viewed as a set of *basic beliefs* (or metaphysics) that deals with ultimates or first principles," and how "[t]he beliefs are basic in the sense that they must be accepted simply on faith (however well argued); there is no way to establish their ultimate truthfulness."[57] I find these words to be extremely relevant to my research, because they're in direct contravention of what I was told by the two white professors and the MBA-holder at Trent University. They argued to me that an Indigenous paradigm did not exist and maintained that their paradigms were the only legitimate ones. Yet of course Indigenous paradigms exist, and are just as relevant as their

55 Egon G. Guba and Yvonna S. Lincoln, "Competing Paradigms in Qualitative Research," in *Handbook of Qualitative Research*, Norman K. Denzin & Yvonna S. Lincoln, eds. (Thousand Oaks: Sage Publishing, 1994), 106.

56 Guba and Lincoln, "Competing Paradigms in Qualitative Research," 109.

57 Guba and Lincoln, "Competing Paradigms in Qualitative Research," 107.

proposed paradigms—more so in my opinion, considering that I am an Indigenous researcher conducting W̱SÁNEĆ research. In this case, my perspective and worldview take precedence over theirs; that is the fatal flaw in their proposed logic. Not only did they consider their worldviews to be the only valid options, but then they tried to impose them on me. Meanwhile, according to Guba and Lincoln, their preferred paradigms are not absolutes but basic beliefs that I was expected to accept on faith.

According to Guba and Lincoln, questions related to ontology, epistemology, axiology, and methodology are answered differently by, and therefore can be used to define, individual paradigms. Questions relate to ways of being, ways of knowing, and ways of doing research. However, Guba and Lincoln point out that "the sets of answers given are in *all* cases *human constructions;* that is, they are all inventions of the human mind and hence subject to human error."[58] I reiterate my previous question of why the two white professors and the MBA-holder were so desperate for me to submit to their way of thinking. This is an especially interesting question considering Guba and Lincoln's statement that "[n]o construction is or can be incontrovertibly right; advocates of any particular construction must rely on *persuasiveness* and *utility* rather than *proof* in arguing their position."[59] Perhaps the questions and statements I made that day during the proposal presentation went unanswered because there were no answers—because ultimately there is no proof, only theories.

Guba and Lincoln display a self-awareness and humility that I found lacking in these Trent academics. Guba and Lincoln write that "[w]hat is true of paradigms is true of our analyses as well. Everything that we shall say subsequently is *also* a human construction: ours."[60] I find this to be an indication of their commitment

58 Guba and Lincoln, "Competing Paradigms in Qualitative Research," 108. Emphasis in original.

59 Guba and Lincoln, "Competing Paradigms in Qualitative Research," 108. Emphasis in original.

60 Guba and Lincoln, "Competing Paradigms in Qualitative Research," 108.

to ethical scholarship, and to their ability to admit their ignorance, which in turn allows for them to be open to more learning and growth. They go so far as to admit that "[t]he reader cannot be compelled to accept our analyses, or our arguments, on the basis of incontestable logic or indisputable evidence; we can only hope to be persuasive and to demonstrate the utility of our position for, say, the public policy arena."[61] There is a vast difference between acting as an agent of capture and *hoping to be persuasive.* Guba and Lincoln are true thinkers and real educators whose approach indicates will not try to impose their worldviews upon others.

However, the main criticism I have of Guba and Lincoln's 1994 article relates to its characterization of the category of critical theory. The criticism also serves as a wider critique for the social sciences in general. Critical theory, as articulated by Guba and Lincoln, serves as a catch-all descriptor for alternative paradigms that do not fit within the other three categories. Additionally, this then serves as a point from which those alternative knowledges can be captured and encompassed, furthering the goal of restructuring proposed by the Gulbenkian Commission report. This is somewhat addressed when they write "that except for positivism, the paradigms discussed are all still in formative stages; no final agreements have been reached even among their proponents about their definitions, meanings, or implications."[62] This idea was inspiring for my writing approach, and specifically for this chapter, which is devoted to using Shawn Wilson's *Research is Ceremony* to establish an Indigenous/W̱SÁNEĆ paradigm.

John Heron and Peter Reason wrote "A Participatory Inquiry Paradigm" in 1997 in response to Guba and Lincoln's article. Guba and Lincoln had situated participatory inquiry under the blanket term "Critical Theory et al." along with feminism, Marxism, etc. Heron and Reason sought to articulate a standalone participatory inquiry paradigm alongside positivism, post-positivism, critical

61 Guba and Lincoln, "Competing Paradigms in Qualitative Research," 108.
62 Guba and Lincoln, "Competing Paradigms in Qualitative Research," 109.

theory, and constructivism. I find much of Heron and Reason's article to be too philosophical and leaning toward what Guba and Lincoln would call "persuasiveness" and "utility." However, there is much in Heron and Reason that I found relevant to my research.

According to Heron and Reason, "participatory inquiry" is itself a blanket term, and additional forms include action inquiry, participatory action research, and emancipatory action research, among others. In fact, scholars Orlando Fals-Borda and Md Anisur Rahman "reported that some 35 varieties of participative action inquiry have been identified worldwide."[63] It is worth noting that this article, along with several others published by Heron and Reason, articulate their preferred form of participatory inquiry, "cooperative inquiry." The timing of these publications aligns nicely with the meetings of the Gulbenkian Commission in 1994–1995 and the subsequent publication of the Gulbenkian Report in 1995. At a time when the Social Science Research Council was positing ways to restructure the social sciences, this participatory inquiry paradigm would seem to have been an ideal response and solution. The main critique I have of this paradigm is the ambiguity of the methodology. It is almost as if the authors cast the net too wide so that they may include as many alternative knowledge systems as possible. There are too many end goals, and not enough explanation of how Heron and Reason arrived at them.

The biggest question posed in this article does not even come from Heron and Reason, as they write: "Denzin and Lincoln (1994) have drawn our attention to the crisis of legitimation in qualitative research, which asks by what right researchers claim to speak for the people they have studied."[64] The problem becomes more pronounced when one considers which paradigm influences

63 Orlando Fals-Borda and Md Anisur Rahman, *Action and Knowledge: Breaking the Monopoly With Participatory Action-Research* (New York / London: Apex Press, 1991), as cited in John Heron and Peter Reason, "A Participatory Inquiry Paradigm," *Qualitative Inquiry* 3, 3 (1997), 284.

64 Heron and Reason, "A Participatory Inquiry Paradigm," 285.

researchers, and the subsequent related issue of a positivist mindset. Continuing this thought process, Heron and Reason state:

> A basic problem of positivist mind is that it cannot acknowledge the framing paradigm it has created. It confuses the given cosmos with the worldview it has generated to shape the given. It cannot see that the ground, on which it stands to frame its world, is its own creation.[65]

The positive aspect found in the generation of a particular worldview recalls Walter D. Mignolo and his theory of the development of the disciplines, which is centred on the idea that a common language was needed for the enunciators to be able to converse with one another about the enunciated. The negative in this scenario becomes the creation of an enclosed worldview that is territorial and prone to aggressive indoctrination. Guba and Lincoln add that "[i]f an inquiry is to be objective, hypotheses must be stated in ways that are independent of the way in which the facts needed to test them are collected," and then further state "[b]ut it now seems established beyond objection that theories and facts are quite *interdependent*—that is, that facts are facts only within some theoretical framework."[66] These statements affirm once again that social science theories result in self-defined truths, under which the facts are provable only when viewed through specific theoretical lenses. Then again, to echo Guba and Lincoln, the facts are less *proof* and more of a *persuasive* argument.

The main issue with Indigenous research is captured in the following Heron and Reason quote: "Qualitative research *about* people is a halfway house between exclusive, controlling, quantitative, positivist research *on* people and fully participatory, cooperative research *with* people."[67] This is an evergreen issue

65 Heron and Reason, "A Participatory Inquiry Paradigm," 275.
66 Guba and Lincoln, "Competing Paradigms in Qualitative Research," 107.
67 Heron and Reason, "A Participatory Inquiry Paradigm," 285.

for Indigenous nations, groups, and organizations. Outsiders come in and their only objective is the acquisition of data. Therefore:

> The great majority of its projects are still unilaterally shaped by the researchers, however emergent that shape may be, however much informed consent is sought, and however much the researchers may be concerned to check their findings with informants' views.[68]

Even if the researchers commit to a more participatory research inquiry in theory, "[i]n practice, it may be reduced to no more than seeking fully informed consent of all informants to the researcher's pre-existent or emerging operational plan" and if that is not sufficient, then "to modifying the plan to obtain such consent."[69] Heron and Reason put forth cooperative inquiry, their preferred form of participatory inquiry paradigm, as the answer to this monumental and recurring problem with Indigenous research in academia.

The problem with their proposition is the academy itself. The notion of any research project in which there is complete cooperation from inception to inscription is preposterous and naïve. I grew up within the W̱SÁNEĆ Nation and could not possibly be more of an insider to my people, and yet I still struggle with issues of accountability to the Nation while also attempting to produce scholarly work that meets the demands of academia. Therefore, the idea that an outsider can come in and work with Indigenous people, and that their work is going to be for Indigenous people and not the academy is frankly laughable. It is far more realistic to have academic goals to work with rearguard intellectuals and post-abyssal knowledges with the intent of delinking through epistemic disobedience than it is to think outsiders are going to come with extractive research goals and that they will produce something other than more social science interpretations of Indigenous Knowledges.

68 Heron and Reason, "A Participatory Inquiry Paradigm," 285.
69 Heron and Reason, "A Participatory Inquiry Paradigm," 285.

This is the main critique I have with Heron and Reason's participatory inquiry paradigm, and why I view it with skepticism considering Wallerstein's Gulbenkian Report. On the one hand, I am leery of a paradigm trying too hard to pull alternative knowledges in under the auspices of the social sciences. However, it cannot ever be a bad thing for researchers to attempt to work collaboratively with Indigenous groups and peoples with a goal of sharing agency and voice throughout the entire research process. However naïve I feel it may be, Heron and Reason's hope that a participatory paradigm will lead to "enabling a balance between people of hierarchy, cooperation, and autonomy" is laudable.[70] Unfortunately, in my experience, the academy is not a very cooperative or accommodating entity. The two white professors and the MBA-holder I mentioned might be more in line with the darker side of the dichotomy established by Heron and Reason:

> The shadow face of authority is authoritarianism; that of collaboration, peer pressure, and conformity; that of autonomy narcissism, willfulness, and isolation. The challenge is to design institutions that manifest valid forms of these principles, and to finds ways in which they can be maintained in self-correcting and creative tension.[71]

My hope is that the social sciences rhetoric and the cognitive imperialism I experienced at Trent University is open to self-correction. Since leaving the campus and Ontario, I have heard anecdotally that positive changes have occurred. I will conclude this examination of Heron and Reason with one final quote:

> There is an urgent need to revision our view of ourselves as coinhabitants of the planet. As many of us have asserted, with greater or lesser degrees of

70 Heron and Reason, "A Participatory Inquiry Paradigm," 287.
71 Heron and Reason, "A Participatory Inquiry Paradigm," 287.

> concern, the current Western worldview has come to the end of its useful life, and, as well as some remarkable achievements in material well-being and human possibility, has left us with a legacy of human alienation and ecological devastation.[72]

It is time to embrace the paradigm shifts currently happening in the academy, Indigenous Studies, and in the social sciences. It is time to acknowledge that there are other worldviews out there—Indigenous worldviews and Indigenous paradigms.

I had expected Guba and Lincoln's subsequent response to Heron and Reason's response to their 1994 article would be a close reading of Heron and Reason, as well as an extension of and expansion upon their original article. I was not entirely wrong. In Guba and Lincoln's 2005 article "Paradigmatic Controversies, Contradictions, and Emerging Confluences," there are pages of tables and many philosophical musings about the shifting paradigm landscape. Guba and Lincoln address a few of the criticisms put forth by Heron and Reason, and they do expand upon the previous article. However, the humility that I noted in the 1994 article, which to me showed their commitment to learning and growing, once again shines through as a ray of hope for the future of Indigenous studies in the academy.

I was initially wary when reading an early quote taken from a 1995 Lincoln article:

> Seven new standards were derived from that research: positionality, or standpoint, judgments; specific discourse communities and research sites as arbiters of quality; voice, or the extent to which a text has the quality of polyvocality; critical subjectivity (or what might be termed intense self-reflexivity); reciprocity, or the extent to which the research relationship

72 Heron and Reason, "A Participatory Inquiry Paradigm," 291.

> becomes reciprocal rather than hierarchical; sacredness, or the profound regard for how science can (and does) contribute to human flourishing; and sharing the perquisites of privilege that accrue to our positions as academics with university positions. Each of these standards was extracted from a body of research, often from disciplines as disparate as management, philosophy, and women's studies.[73]

I was wary because this paragraph reeks of Wallerstein's proposal to open the social sciences to subsume alternative knowledges. However, I once again underestimated the openness to new possibilities and learning that Guba and Lincoln display.

Rather than attempting to assimilate alternative knowledges within the social sciences, Guba and Lincoln instead acknowledge the changes happening within social science research itself:

> For purposes of this discussion, we believe the adoption of the most radical definitions of social science are appropriate, because the paradigmatic controversies are often taking place at the edges of those conversations. Those edges are where the border work is occurring, and, accordingly, they are the places that show the most promise for projecting where qualitative methods will be in the near and far future.[74]

This paragraph gave me a renewed faith that not all social sciences researchers have a narrow and limited worldview, and that there do exist non-Indigenous social scientists who can see the future of embracing all research. My experiences at Trent would fall under

73 Yvonna S. Lincoln and Egon G. Guba, "Paradigmatic Controversies, Contradictions, and Emerging Confluences," in *The SAGE Handbook of Qualitative Research*, Norman K. Denzin, Yvonna S. Lincoln, eds. (Thousand Oaks: Sage Publications, 2005), 192.

74 Lincoln and Guba, "Paradigmatic Controversies, Contradictions, and Emerging Confluences," 179.

what Guba and Lincoln term "a crisis of representation (which serves to silence those whose lives we appropriate for our social sciences, and which may also serve subtly to re-create *this* world, rather than some other, perhaps more complex, but just one)."[75] I will never understand the attempt to silence me rather than to accept the unavoidable paradigm shifts. All that is required is a shift in accepting alternate worldviews, and we could re-create a more just academic world.

Guba and Lincoln are inspirational and affirmational in their quest for learning and growth. They are open to new possibilities in ways I did not encounter at Trent University:

> Representation may be arguably the most open-ended of the controversies surrounding phenomenological research today, for no other reasons than that the ideas of what constitutes legitimate inquiry are expanding and, at the same time, the forms of narrative, dramatic, and rhetorical structure are far from being either explored or exploited fully. Because, too, each inquiry, each inquirer, brings a unique perspective to our understanding, the possibilities for variation and exploration are limited only by the number of those engaged in inquiry and the realms of social and intrapersonal life that become interesting to researchers.[76]

I hate to add anything to the already perfect words of these preeminent social science scholars, especially something negative. However, researchers are also limited by those in charge of the institutions, programs, and departments. Those currently in charge have the capacity to cause a great deal of damage to the trajectory and progress of researchers who are supposed to be under their

75 Lincoln and Guba, "Paradigmatic Controversies, Contradictions, and Emerging Confluences," 184.

76 Lincoln and Guba, "Paradigmatic Controversies, Contradictions, and Emerging Confluences," 185.

guidance. If they act out of ego or petty narcissistic retaliation, they have the power to delay and/or disrupt research. Instead, I hope they choose to be a part of a positive change toward a new and more just academic world.

In keeping with the outlook of Guba and Lincoln, I would like to finish with one final quote from this surprising and inspiring social science article:

> At some distance down this conjectural path, when its history is written, we will find that this has been the era of emancipation: emancipation from what Hannah Arendt calls "the coerciveness of Truth," emancipation from hearing only the voices of Western Europe, emancipation from generations of silence, and emancipation from seeing the world in one color.[77]

I have focused here on the practice of delinking from social science rhetoric and emancipation from the cognitive control of dominant social sciences paradigms. Having established the existence of alternative knowledges and the diversification of social sciences research frameworks, in conjunction with the emergence of alternative knowledges in the inquiry paradigm classifications, I now return to Shawn Wilson's articulation of an Indigenous paradigm.

While taking a first-year course in the Indigenous Studies PhD program at Trent University, I discovered a fundamental difference in research conception between myself and a white professor. The course was titled "Indigenous Studies Theory and Research Methods." The professor asked that we participate in an exercise in which we drew a picture of what we thought a literature review would look like. It was a very simple exercise meant to offer a way of conceptualizing a literature review outside of the standard written format.

77 Lincoln and Guba, "Paradigmatic Controversies, Contradictions, and Emerging Confluences," 185.

The white professor's drawing was typical of a western approach to a literature review. She described it as an introductory paragraph, followed by major ideas surrounding by the corresponding literature references. In her rendering, the major ideas formed one or more paragraphs as needed, and the whole literature review ended with a concluding paragraph. It was the outline of a standard western eurocentric literature review. My drawing depicted a winding path that represented both my life and education journey. Along the journey, major ideas were formed and new materials were added over time. Ultimately the whole path became circular and returned to where it began—the W̱SÁNEĆ Nation. I chose to employ storytelling as methodology, and in fact I began this written assignment with "Storytelling remains an essential part of all Indigenous nations, and for this reason I would like to employ it as method in the first section [of this paper]."[78] I intuited the potential problems as soon as I saw the two contrasting drawings, and so prior to writing the assignment I asked if we were expected to write our papers based on the white professor's example. Their exact words were "We don't prescribe how you write your assignments," and so I wrote mine from an Indigenous storytelling perspective. The first section of my paper was written in the storytelling format, and the second detailed why the white professor's approach did not work for my research. The white professor had stated that she would not prescribe how I was expected to write the assignment, and yet I received a very low grade for not following her format.

One of the most pressing problems with Indigenous Knowledge in the academy is the issue of compartmentalization I wrote about earlier. Had I followed the format that had been suggested (but not required) by the white professor, I would have had to compartmentalize areas of W̱SÁNEĆ living. It is impossible to compartmentalize W̱SÁNEĆ longhouse practices from W̱SÁNEĆ resource gathering and/or W̱SÁNEĆ territory because they are interconnected and

78 Personal communication, seminar assignment, Trent University, fall 2014.

naturally fuse into one another. It would be equally impossible to compartmentalize myself from my research. Compartmentalization is technically possible in both cases; however, the text generated would feel incomplete and lack a true holistic W̱SÁNEĆ authenticity. It would show the same lack of truth as it would if an outsider white researcher—or perhaps a captive mind—had produced it.

It is my contention that this is the biggest challenge facing Indigenous Knowledge in the academy. Guba and Lincoln as well as Heron and Reason use tables when deconstructing the paradigms. They compartmentalize ontology, epistemology, axiology, and methodology before deconstructing each individually. Shawn Wilson in *Research is Ceremony* instead utilizes a circle when articulating ontology, epistemology, axiology, and methodology. Wilson does this because "the elements of an Indigenous research paradigm are interrelated or interdependent; it is difficult to separate one to write about," and because "there is no distinction between where one element ends and the next begins."[79] The same issues arise when considering the compartmentalization inherent in the white professor's concept of a literature review from an Indigenous perspective. It does not work for us, and for me, it recalls Leroy Little Bear's "Jagged Worldviews Colliding." I cannot separate myself from my W̱SÁNEĆ Indigeneity.

Relationality is a vital concept in an Indigenous paradigm. In *Research as Ceremony*, Wilson writes:

> Relationality seems to sum up the whole Indigenous research paradigm to me. Just as the components of the paradigm are related, the components themselves all have to do with relationships. The ontology and epistemology are based upon a process of relationships that form a mutual reality. The axiology and methodology are based upon maintaining accountability to these relationships.[80]

79 Wilson, *Research is Ceremony*, 69.
80 Wilson, *Research is Ceremony*, 70-71.

Here we begin to see a solution put forth by Wilson. No longer should we compartmentalize Indigenous ways of being (ontology), ways of knowing (epistemology), and ways of doing (axiology and methodology) by dissecting the pieces of ourselves and our nations so that we can feed that all back to the university in a format deemed acceptable to it. The holistic relationality of an Indigenous paradigm is in contradiction to, and therefore prevents, research that dissects and compartmentalizes.

Indigenous researchers have always had to contend with systemic eurocentric western institutional racism and its proponents. Shawn Wilson writes that:

> [a]s proponents of a holistic view of our worlds, Indigenous scholars may recognize the holistic approach to oppression that is evident in all of the ways that Indigenous Peoples are held down by research and the dominant view of knowledge and the world is upheld.[81]

It follows, then, that the holistic approach inherent in an Indigenous paradigm is the antidote to the holistic approach of oppression from those who would harass us. Relationality holds the key, or as Wilson states, "[f]rom an epistemology and ontology based upon relationships, an indigenous methodology and axiology emerge. An indigenous axiology is built upon a concept of relational accountability."[82] I am an Indigenous, W̱SÁNEĆ researcher, and if I am truly working from a holistic, Indigenous, W̱SÁNEĆ paradigm, then those relational accountabilities extend far beyond the bounds of a standard ethics approval within the university system.

I have heard Leanne Betasamosake Simpson say on a few occasions that university thinkers think from the neck up. I would add that most often, their heads are firmly placed within the hallowed halls of the ivory tower. Therefore, they fail to grasp the

81 Wilson, *Research is Ceremony*, 17.
82 Wilson, *Research is Ceremony*, 77.

importance of our responsibilities as Indigenous researchers. When these tower-heads go out and do "Indigenous" research, they are visiting our lands and peoples for data. Then they take that data back to the hallowed halls of the ivory tower and they work on it there—from the neck up. Wilson writes:

> if the importance of relationships were understood at an inner or core level by dominant system researchers and academics, I wouldn't have witnessed the misunderstandings and resistance to an Indigenous research paradigm in connection with my own work and that of other Indigenous researchers.[83]

The fierce opposition to my proposed research is exactly why I have had to address the issue of an Indigenous paradigm within my research.

When I write about the W̱SÁNEĆ Nation, I am not writing about W̱SÁNEĆ data. This is not data that I extracted from my nation and people to think about from the neck up so that I could then produce a boring social science dissertation. I embodied W̱SÁNEĆ living. I grew up running barefoot on our lands and swimming naked in our seas. I travelled and fished among our islands and ran up our sacred ȽÁU, WELṈEW̱ mountain to ceremonially bathe in the running stream, the way my ancestors have done since time immemorial. I have buried countless relatives in the W̱SÁNEĆ grounds the way my ancestors have done since time immemorial. My research question is this: How do I, a W̱SÁNEĆ artist and academic, utilize embodied W̱SÁNEĆ Knowledge in my artistic and academic work? Three tower-heads with no concept of good and ethical Indigenous research were in no position to judge how I answer that question.

I have established that Indigenous Knowledge has always existed outside of the eurocentric western knowledge-making systems. I have established that there are scholars writing against the

83 Wilson, *Research is Ceremony*, 79.

social sciences with the intent of revealing alternative knowledge systems. I have established how social science paradigms have been changing and shifting since at least 2005. Since that point, the social sciences have been open to alternative knowledges as a part of their paradigms. I have established that an Indigenous paradigm has always existed and that it is therefore completely acceptable for me to utilize an Indigenous/W̱SÁNEĆ paradigm in my research. Finally, an Indigenous paradigm requires relationality at its core. Ways of being—(ontology), ways of knowing (epistemology), and ways of doing (axiology and methodology)—must be interrelated and blend into one another. Therefore, embodied W̱SÁNEĆ Knowledge takes the form of practices on the land, spiritual and cultural activities, story, songs, dances, and longhouse activities. All are vital components of a W̱SÁNEĆ paradigm. Finally, embodied W̱SÁNEĆ Knowledge should no longer be a contested concept in academic research.

Shawn Wilson quotes the three R's as articulated by Cora Weber-Pillwax. They are: respect, reciprocity, and responsibility.[84] Wilson and Weber-Pillwax are referring to the relationship of the researcher with an Indigenous research community or group. However, these relational concepts also apply to non-Indigenous groups and places as well—places such as universities, for example. Wilson writes:

> So the presentation or knowledge transfer is again all about continuing healthy relationships. Having a relationship with an idea also means that you must honour and respect that idea. The environment where the idea is to be discussed or further built upon must be appropriately developed and maintained. A healthy relationship cannot be built or flourish in an unhealthy environment.[85]

84 Cora Weber-Pillwax, "What is Indigenous Research?" *Canadian Journal of Native Education* 25, 2 (2001): 166–174.

85 Wilson, *Research is Ceremony*, 125.

If tower-heads gang up on Indigenous students and repeatedly question the legitimacy of their research, they are not creating a healthy environment. Their very own social sciences scholars have been producing work since at least 2005 that would accept research such as mine under their expanded paradigms. However, because of Shawn Wilson's research before me, I can confidently assert an Indigenous/W̱SÁNEĆ paradigm. Therefore, the acceptance of social science advocates and their social sciences paradigms is a only a secondary concern at best. The core of my dissertation research, and the book you are reading now, is a resolute move away from the cognitive imperialism of the social sciences.

As I've established, embodied W̱SÁNEĆ Knowledge and experiental W̱SÁNEĆ Knowledge transfer are key components in pre-contact W̱SÁNEĆ teaching and learning. The traditional W̱SÁNEĆ longhouse (or bighouse), and multi-generational family structure aid in a community engagement at all ages and levels of teaching and learning. The embodied W̱SÁNEĆ Knowledge transfer through experiental W̱SÁNEĆ teaching and learning that formed the ways of being (ontology), ways of knowing (epistemology), and ways of doing (axiology and methodology) for the W̱SÁNEĆ People and that is a key component of the W̱SÁNEĆ paradigm, is what contact and colonization worked so hard to destroy. Once the W̱SÁNEĆ women realized the impact of residential schools and that the Tsartlip Indian Day School was there to stay, they worked hard to bring the Saanich Indian School Board into existence. The W̱SÁNEĆ women inserted themselves into the Tsartlip Indian Day School education process and thus made sure to keep an Indigenous connection between themselves and the W̱SÁNEĆ children in the face of the non-Indigenous teaching pedagogy. These early efforts of the W̱SÁNEĆ women created an oasis of teaching and learning, bridging the gap between traditional W̱SÁNEĆ Knowledge and the demands of colonial education.

When a W̱SÁNEĆ community member is brought into our longhouse traditions, their family stands with them on the floor of our longhouse. They stand behind them, and then further behind stand our W̱SÁNEĆ ancestors, stretching back through time. The support is endless. This is the support I felt even during the darkest times in my graduate studies. It comes from my ancestors standing behind me, as well as from Walter D. Mignolo, Syed Farid Alatas, Syed Hussein Alatas, Bonaventura de Sousa Santos, Leanne Betasamosake Simpson, and Shawn Wilson. These scholars have carved out a path in the academy and fought early battles—some of which I continue to fight today. But I am still here, and I am still writing. TOL, NEW̱ SEN TŦE SOȽ—I know the road.

I know the road because of those who have walked it before me.

With an Indigenous/W̱SÁNEĆ paradigm established, we must next examine the components that make up what it means to be W̱SÁNEĆ. Because traditional W̱SÁNEĆ Knowledge transfer involved many activities and practices on W̱SÁNEĆ lands and seas, the embodiment of those practices held the key to W̱SÁNEĆ survival. Through embodied teaching and learning we not only survived but thrived and lived a privileged existence prior to contact and colonization. Embodied W̱SÁNEĆ Knowledge as a concept, along with traditional W̱SÁNEĆ story, culture and traditions are what I'll now explore in detail.

EMBODIED W̱SÁNEĆ KNOWLEDGE

I began to research embodied knowledge through the York University library research portal, and I was caught off guard by how broad the use of the term was. For the most part, conceptions of embodied knowledge were literal. These were reminiscent of the perspectives of the graduate students in the media studies seminar I attended at York who could not conceive of a collective group knowledge where learning and teaching occur without the use of books, and thus asked the question of whether embodied knowledge was kept in an arm or leg. Over at Trent University I had been similarly challenged with the question about whether all seminars were embodied because our bodies were present in the seminar room. For a seminar to be considered embodied, one would have to start with the subject the seminar was focused on. Sitting in a room and studying a subject from the neck up is not embodying the subject—that is standard colonial education. However, embodied teaching and learning did occur when our cohort went out on the land to gather and then dance the rice—*that* was embodying rice gathering knowledge. Then when that same cohort went out on the land and tapped the maple trees for sap and then boiled that sap down to make syrup—*that* was embodying sugarbush knowledge. There is a huge difference between the practices of dancing the rice and working in the sugarbush, and the practice of sitting in the seminar room at Trent University while listening to a lecture about grounded theory. We were not embodying a seminar about grounded theory. Our mind and bodies were indeed present, but ultimately this was passive listening at best. Embodied Indigenous Knowledge is not placing the body of a person in a place or a situation and then announcing that that place or situation is embodied. There is far more to it than that.

The definitions I found for embodied knowledge were informative and they instructed how I came to define research about embodied Indigenous Knowledge. For example, in "From Embedded Knowledge to Embodied Knowledge," embodied knowledge is literally the embedded knowledge (idea) in physical form—the product of research and development.[86] The entire article is dedicated to the most efficient practices for developing research and ideas from conception to product. Similarly, most of the article "Embodied Knowledge and Sectoral Linkages," was incomprehensible to me because of its research area specificity. What I found interesting were the authors' use of industry terms "R&D embodied," "embodied technology," and "product-embodied."[87] The article examines cost-efficiencies for multiple countries and industries in creating a product, and the cost of shipping the components for construction and the final product to the consumer. Once again, "embodied" here refers to a product or the product parts, a framing that is very capitalist. The definitions and uses of embodied knowledge I discovered in my research were far too numerous and none proved useful for me to engage with. It was therefore necessary to move on from embodied knowledge research that was *not* relevant to my research, and instead focus on the criteria and definition of embodied Indigenous Knowledge.

86 Ravindranath Madhavan and Rajiv Grover, "From Embedded Knowledge to Embodied Knowledge: New Product Development as Knowledge Management," *Journal of Marketing* 6, 4 (1998).

87 John Hauknes and Mark Knell, "Embodied Knowledge and Sectoral Linkages: Input–output Approach to the Interaction of High- and Low-tech Industries," *Research policy* 38, 3 (2009).

EMBODIED INDIGENOUS KNOWLEDGE

The first thing I did when I began to engage with embodied Indigenous Knowledge was to draw on specific books from our core comprehensive reading list. I began with *Dancing On Our Turtle's Back* by Leanne Betasamosake Simpson because I have read it at least a dozen times, and it remains one of the best examples of authentic Indigenous scholarship. Simpson shares the Nishnaabeg Creation Story in the section "Embodied Knowledge, Unlimited Intelligence," in which she writes:

> The next part of the story, after Gzhwe Mnidoo has lowered me to the earth, tells us that Gzhwe Mnidoo put her/his right hand to my forehead and s/he transferred all of Gzhwe Mnidoo's thoughts into me. There were so many, that the thoughts couldn't just stay in my head, they spilled into every part of my being and filled up my whole body. Gzhwe Mnidoo's knowledge was so immense from creating the world that it took all of my being to embody it.[88]

When I read that paragraph, it represents a perfect example of embodied Indigenous Knowledge. I could not articulate it any better—but in the following pages I will make an attempt. The reason I must do this is because the social scientists will misunderstand its meaning, context, and validity, and therefore deny that it has any basis in fact. Embodied Indigenous Knowledge is encoded in our stories, our songs, our dances, our practices on the land, our ceremonies, and in everyday living. Embodied Indigenous knowledge is not stored in our brain or in a book—it connects us as Indigenous Peoples to the practice or purpose at hand. It is beyond the scope of the written word and that is where it comes into conflict with contemporary teaching and learning in academia.

88 Leanne Betasamosake Simpson, *Dancing On Our Turtle's Back.*

Reading Simpson's beautiful words, I am reminded of Shawn Wilson's engagement with Cora Weber-Pillwax's three R's: respect, reciprocity, and responsibility. Wilson reminds us that we cannot accomplish our research in a good and healthy way while existing in an unhealthy environment—and this includes the relationship we have with the academy and institutions of study. The unhealthy relationships we have with our institution of study can adversely affect our relationship and responsibilities we have to our Indigenous nations. Those petty criticisms and conflicts distract us from our real work. Similarly, Simpson's words reminded me that the W̱SÁNEĆ Knowledge is already embodied in me, and my experiences at Trent University cannot change that fact. I allowed those experiences to impact my self-perception, and the Nishnaabeg Creation Story reminded me of who I am. I must never forget I am first and foremost a W̱SÁNEĆ community member, after that am I a W̱SÁNEĆ artist, and only then am I an academic.

I will continue to return to Weber-Pillwax's three R's because it is imperative that I remember who I am. I must keep in mind why I am writing and why, all those years ago, while sitting in the library at the University of Victoria, I decided to follow this path. Somewhere during the PhD process, the idea of research for and about the W̱SÁNEĆ Nation became lost in the politics of negotiating the university system. I am not sure that those I came into conflict with understood the seriousness of my commitment to W̱SÁNEĆ research and to the relationship with my family and the W̱SÁNEĆ Nation—which goes above and beyond any university requirements.

> All things are related and therefore relevant. This concept permeates recent scholarly writing by Indigenous scholars. They question whether, in fact, it is even possible for dominant system researchers to understand this concept with the depth that is required for respectful research with Indigenous Peoples.[89]

89 Wilson, *Research is Ceremony*, 58.

When those in charge of the Indigenous Studies PhD program at Trent University attempted to insert themselves into my research and insisted that I change it to suit their worldviews, they demonstrated a lack of commitment to respectful relationships conducted within healthy research environments. The W̱SÁNEĆ paradigm locates W̱SÁNEĆ Knowledge outside of the framework of their comfortable university environment, and this was the main source of the problem. It is unavoidable.

I know from Wilson's excellent book that compartmentalization of W̱SÁNEĆ ways of being (ontology), W̱SÁNEĆ ways of knowing (epistemology), and W̱SÁNEĆ ways of doing (axiology and methodology) becomes problematic because in our worldview these attributes do not exist in a western linear continuum. Instead, they exist in a circular pattern, interrelated and fused with one another. Wilson writes:

> From an epistemology and ontology based upon relationships, an indigenous methodology and axiology emerge. An indigenous axiology is built upon a concept of relational accountability. Right or wrong; validity; statistically significant; worthy or unworthy: value judgments lose their meaning. What is more important and meaningful is fulfilling a role and obligations in the research relationship - that is, being accountable to your relations.[90]

So being accountable to my W̱SÁNEĆ relations was the most important aspect of my PhD dissertation work. Whichever conflicts and contestations I encountered within the University system along the journey toward my doctorate—that point was non-negotiable. The depth of W̱SÁNEĆ responsibility for this researcher is immense.

W̱SÁNEĆ ways of being, knowing, and doing, are best articulated as a circular construct with no beginning and no end point. The attributes are interrelated and therefore difficult to separate and

90 Wilson, *Research is Ceremony*, 77.

deconstruct, meaning that one cannot start with ontology and work one's way through to epistemology, axiology, and finally methodology. The articulation of a W̱SÁNEĆ paradigm is not such a straightforward task. However, the Anishinaabeg Creation Story, as written in Leanne Betasamosake Simpson's book, reminded me of a W̱SÁNEĆ story that I believe is as good place to start. Jumping into the circle that is a W̱SÁNEĆ paradigm starts here.

W̱SÁNEĆ WAYS OF BEING (ONTOLOGY)

When I began to research this section, I returned to some reading sources that I had not read in a while—except this time I read them through the lens of W̱SÁNEĆ ways of being, knowing, and doing. This process made my heart ache, as I longed for the beauty of pre-colonization W̱SÁNEĆ living. I am sad for a life I have never known because colonization has irrevocably altered W̱SÁNEĆ ways of living. In *The Saltwater People*, Dave Elliot Sr. has this to say about W̱SÁNEĆ Peoples:

> We knew there was an intelligence, a strength, a power, far beyond ourselves. We knew that everything here didn't just happen by accident. We believed there was a reason for it being here. There was a force, a strength, a power somewhere that was responsible for it. That is the way our people lived. They lived according to that belief, according to that knowledge.[91]

I relied heavily on *The Saltwater People*, and on *ÁLENENEC: Learning From Homeland*, and *The Saanich Year* while writing this section.[92] *ÁLENENEC* was self-published by the Saanich Adult

91 Dave Elliot Sr., *The Saltwater People*, 75.

92 W̱SÁNEĆ Community members, *ÁLENENEC: Learning From Homeland* (Saanich: Saanich Adult Education Centre, Saanich Indian School Board, 2008); Earle Claxton and John Elliott, *The Saanich Year* (Saanich: Saanich School Board, 1993), booklet #63.

Education Centre and the Saanich Indian School Board in consultation with the SAEC Cultural and Research Advisory Council and members of the W̱SÁNEĆ community. Dave Elliot's son John Elliot was one of the contributors for this W̱SÁNEĆ community project.

XÁLS (Creator) gave the W̱SÁNEĆ a beautiful place to live, and we had an abundance of everything we needed. XÁLS placed the first W̱SÁNEĆ person down in what would become the most ancient of W̱SÁNEĆ village sites, called SṈIDȻEŁ. SṈIDȻEŁ means "place of blue grouse" because they were once plentiful in that area. SṈIDȻEŁ was stolen from the W̱SÁNEĆ Peoples. It is the area around what is now called the Todd Inlet and includes the world-famous tourist attraction called the Butchart Gardens. SLEMEW̱ (Rain) was the first W̱SÁNEĆ person placed down at SṈIDȻEŁ, and there they learned to live with some additional W̱SÁNEĆ relatives, SMÍEŦ (deer) and SĆÁÁNEW̱ (Salmon). One day, XÁLS gathered three black pebbles and threw them, and where they landed, three large mountains grew. One of those mountains was our sacred ŁÁU, WELṈEW̱ and another was PKOLS (the colonizers named it Mount Doug). XÁLS went to the top of the mountain and the W̱SÁNEĆ Peoples followed him. He then took some of the W̱SÁNEĆ People and tossed them into the waters where they changed into islands. XÁLS instructed the W̱SÁNEĆ Peoples to take care of their island relatives and for the island relatives to take care of the W̱SÁNEĆ Peoples. Therefore, those islands are collectively referred to as TETÁCES—Relatives of the deep. These were some of the relatives to the W̱SÁNEĆ Peoples, and we all lived in harmony and took care of one another.[93]

The giant cedar trees once lived among the W̱SÁNEĆ Peoples, and because of their great size they would sometimes forget themselves and hurt the W̱SÁNEĆ people. XÁLS would become angry with them and scold them, after which they would behave for a short while. But soon enough they would forget again and hurt

93 W̱SÁNEĆ Community members, Saanich Adult Education Centre et al, *ÁLENENEC*, 2008.

one of the W̱SÁNEĆ Peoples. The last time they did this, they tried to run away from XÁLS, and he made their feet stick to the ground because he turned them into the roots of the cedar tree. Ever since then, the cedar trees have taken care of the W̱SÁNEĆ Peoples and provided us with many gifts. These relatives are called SKELALNEW, which means "the bad ones put away." W̱SÁNEĆ Peoples always give thanks to our cedar relatives when we use one of their gifts.[94]

As can be seen in the words of Dave Elliot Sr., we lived according to the knowledge that we were created along with our surroundings. W̱SÁNEĆ Peoples have lived in our territories since time immemorial and we are related to the trees, the animals, the mountains, and the islands. It was this holistic, balanced understanding that formed the core of our being as a people. The W̱SÁNEĆ Peoples still had conflicts with our northern neighbours, such as the time the ancient village site SṈIDȻEȽ was attacked. Eventually, some of the W̱SÁNEĆ Peoples moved over to the village areas now call WJOLEP and TSAWOUT, where two of our reserve areas are still located today. It is said that at the time the Douglas Treaty was signed between James Douglas and the W̱SÁNEĆ Peoples there were 7,000 of us living in the ancient village SṈIDȻEȽ.[95]

Contained in the wording of the Douglas Treaty with the W̱SÁNEĆ Peoples was the provision we could continue to hunt and fish as before. The W̱SÁNEĆ Peoples were ravaged by disease, and as a result our population, and therefore our ability to defend our territory, was affected. To save the area around SṈIDȻEȽ, the W̱SÁNEĆ Peoples fenced it off and kept animals there. One year, when my people left the area to assist with reef-net fishing, the colonizers removed the fences and began building on that land. They just moved in and took the land, and the W̱SÁNEĆ

94 W̱SÁNEĆ Community members, Saanich Adult Education Centre et al, *ÁLENENEC*, 2008.

95 W̱SÁNEĆ Community members, Saanich Adult Education Centre et al, *ÁLENENEC*, 2008.

Peoples, reduced by disease and outnumbered, could do nothing about it. The entire W̱SÁNEĆ territories once encompassed what is now called the Saanich Peninsula and the surrounding islands. Currently, the four remaining W̱SÁNEĆ reserve areas amount to a small fraction of the original W̱SÁNEĆ territories. Our reserves are surrounded by non-Indigenous homes, businesses, and municipalities. W̱SÁNEĆ lands have been irrevocably changed, but our connection to our relations remains strong. W̱SÁNEĆ Peoples have been there ever since XÁLS placed the first W̱SÁNEĆ person, SLEMEW̱, down in that most ancient of village sites, SṈIDȻEȽ. We were there when XÁLS created ȽÁU, WELṈEW̱, the sacred mountain that saved us after the great flood, and the same mountain I ran up when I was initiated as a traditional W̱SÁNEĆ longhouse dancer. W̱SÁNEĆ ways of being are intertwined with all of this and more, and no amount of colonization can alter our story and our connection to W̱SÁNEĆ territory.[96]

W̱SÁNEĆ WAYS OF KNOWING (EPISTEMOLOGY)

There were once many W̱SÁNEĆ ways of knowing that defined us as W̱SÁNEĆ Peoples. After colonization we gradually lost access to most of our traditional practices. The ancient W̱SÁNEĆ longhouse traditions were affected by the legislation passed by the Government of Canada forbidding the practice of the potlatch, beginning in 1885 and lasting until 1951. During that time, our practices never stopped, but instead were carried on in secret. The W̱SÁNEĆ winter dances are one of the few traditional W̱SÁNEĆ practices that has remained relatively unchanged since time immemorial. It was a cathartic experience for me to join the ancestors who came before me and to become initiated as a traditional W̱SÁNEĆ longhouse dancer in 2009. I entered this vital and life-changing experience and became a traditional W̱SÁNEĆ longhouse dancer at the age of forty-two,

96 W̱SÁNEĆ Community members, Saanich Adult Education Centre et al, *ÁLENENEC*, 2008.

and it fundamentally shifted how I move through the world. The process was extremely difficult, and though I did my best to prepare, I was inevitably pushed to my very limits. Once I had completed the process, I was connected as a W̱SÁNEĆ person to all those W̱SÁNEĆ new dancers who had come before me, stretching back in time generation after generation. It remains one of the most incredible experiences of my life. As a result, I am a W̱SÁNEĆ traditional dancer, and I represent my nation and my family in everything I do. This is not a task I take lightly.

At the end of approximately five days of initiation, a new dancer is presented to the community in a ceremony. Prior to that day it will have been a small group of individuals and the family of the initiate who have been observing and aiding in the work. On the presentation night, I recall feeling certain that I was in a huge arena and that there was row upon row of people stretching far up into the sky who were watching the ceremony. When I later relayed my perception of the experience to my sister, she said that it was all the W̱SÁNEĆ ancestors who had danced before me coming to watch. I later discovered that the longhouse I danced in was about the size of a small gymnasium—but what I felt and heard was twenty times the size of that longhouse.

The presentation night is a long and gruelling one, and begins early in the morning with a run up the sacred ŁÁU, WELṈEW̱ mountain to cleanse oneself in its waters. The W̱SÁNEĆ have been conducting this practice over countless generations spanning back through time. On the evening my own presentation ceremony was completed, I recall standing on the floor of the longhouse while my family stood behind me in support. The family stands behind the new dancer to show their support to the wider community. More importantly this shows to the community the responsibility the new dancer has to their family and in this act, the new dancer becomes representative in their deeds and actions to both their family and the entire W̱SÁNEĆ community. This is the responsibility that I have accepted willingly, and do not take lightly. As of that moment,

I became truly W̱SÁNEĆ, and now forever represent my family and the W̱SÁNEĆ community. I must never forget the sacrifices my family and the community made for me to have that honour.

Once the new dancer has been presented and everyone has been thanked, the new dancer and their family remain on the floor. This is when experienced W̱SÁNEĆ dancers and those dancers visiting from other communities are allowed to take the floor and offer words of advice to guide the new dancer in their new life. This allows for teachings to be passed from the older dancers to the new dancer and it's the perfect opportunity for important teachings to be shared between Indigenous nations and communities. One of the people to stand up and come and speak to me was a 105-year-old man who was helped onto the floor by his great-granddaughter. He spoke only SENĆOŦEN, and his great-granddaughter translated. He talked about what it was like when he was a young boy and became a new dancer. He told the story of how he lived in one of three longhouses side by side, and told me about the process of waking up early every morning, when all the new dancers would go from one longhouse to the next and dance. He then talked about how our longhouse dancing practices have remained with us through time. Whatever else happens in the outside world, when we come into our longhouses, we are doing things the way our W̱SÁNEĆ ancestors have always done. The world outside continues to change, and yet inside our longhouses, our traditions remain and integral part of W̱SÁNEĆ ways of knowing. I was humbled and awestruck by this Elder and his words.

W̱SÁNEĆ WAYS OF DOING (AXIOLOGY AND METHODOLOGY)

Shawn Wilson is correct in that an Indigenous paradigm, and by extension a W̱SÁNEĆ paradigm, has elements that are relational, interrelated, and predicated upon relational accountability to keep them in balance. I can think of no better example of relational accountability than the W̱SÁNEĆ practice of SX̱OLE (reef-net fishing). Nicholas Xemtoltw Claxton has written extensively about the W̱SÁNEĆ Peoples and SX̱OLE. Much of this section has been gleaned from his incredible research for his MA and then PhD at the University of Victoria in 2003 and 2015.[97]

The W̱SÁNEĆ practice of SX̱OLE was developed through a process of scientific experimental trial and error. There is no other way this incredibly complex activity with so many diverse components could have come to exist. Expert knowledge was obtained through embodied W̱SÁNEĆ Knowledge transfer in diverse areas like astrology, to know where the stars are in relation to when the different species of SĆÁÁNEW̱ would arrive; botany, to know the best time of year to gather the multiple materials used in the construction of the SX̱OLE; oceanography, to have a thorough understanding of the tides and how ocean currents will affect the SĆÁÁNEW̱ swimming patterns; and finally climatology to be sure the weather is safe to engage in this all-encompassing endeavour. However, before I delve into any specific interrelated components and their subsequent relational accountabilities, I will present the W̱SÁNEĆ teaching about SĆÁÁNEW̱ (the salmon).

Recall I wrote that all our relatives lived in harmony with the first person, SLEMEW̱, after he was placed in the ancient village site of SṈIDȻEŁ. One community of our relatives lived a good life—they worked hard, and were always there to help others. XÁLS saw this and one day rewarded them by turning them into SĆÁÁNEW̱ (SĆÁ means "working," while NEW̱ means "people"). The SĆÁÁNEW̱ work hard each year, travelling to return to W̱SÁNEĆ spawning grounds. Along the way, the SĆÁÁNEW̱ help their relatives, including the W̱SÁNEĆ Peoples. The different types of SĆÁÁNEW̱ arrive at different times during the summer, and represent four distinct family groups among the SĆÁÁNEW̱ Peoples. Just like the

97 Additional research about SX̱OLE in this section has been gleaned from *Saltwater People* (Elliot Sr., 1983) and *ÁLENENEC: Learning from Homeland* (SAEC, 2008).

surrounding islands, the birds, and the trees, the SĆÁÁNEW̱ are our relatives, and we honour them as such.[98]

Claxton relates another story of our SĆÁÁNEW̱ ancestors and how they gifted us with the SX̱OLE. There once was a young W̱SÁNEĆ woman who would go and sit by herself on the beach. One day, a handsome young man came and asked if he could join her. They visited like this for several days and because she was traditional, she asked if he would meet her parents. At the time, the W̱SÁNEĆ Peoples were hungry and didn't know about the practice using SX̱OLE. The parents gave their blessing to the union, but before the young man agreed, he asked them to bring him some materials. One by one he asked for each article needed for the creation of the SX̱OLE, and then he showed them how to build and to use it. The W̱SÁNEĆ Peoples were happy, and when they were finished the young man took the young W̱SÁNEĆ woman and they return to his home with the SĆÁÁNEW̱ People. Now, every year, when the SĆÁÁNEW̱ first return to the W̱SÁNEĆ Peoples, a celebration is made. The first salmon is cooked and eaten, and the bones are returned to the sea as a prayer offering of thanks to our SĆÁÁNEW̱ relatives.[99]

Because W̱SÁNEĆ ways of being (ontology), W̱SÁNEĆ ways of knowing (epistemology), and W̱SÁNEĆ ways of doing (axiology and methodology) are interrelated and interchangeable, the practices I outlined in each of the previous sections could be taken and placed into any of the others. This is the holistic nature of Indigenous and W̱SÁNEĆ paradigms. However, the construction and utilization of the W̱SÁNEĆ SX̱OLE is of particular interest because it involves every aspect of W̱SÁNEĆ living—ways of being, knowing, and doing. Embodied W̱SÁNEĆ Knowledge

98 Nicholas Xemtoltw Claxton, "To Fish as Formerly: A Resurgent Journey Back to the Saanich Reef Net Fishery," unpublished PhD dissertation, University of Victoria (2015). Retrieved from http://hdl.handle.net/1828/6614.

99 W̱SÁNEĆ Community members, Saanich Adult Education Centre et al, *ÁLENENEC*, 2008.

transfer happens in multiple capacities involving multiple areas of W̱SÁNEĆ living in this practice that articulates the very core of what it means to be W̱SÁNEĆ.

RELATIONAL, INTERRELATED, AND RELATIONAL ACCOUNTABILITY OF W̱SÁNEĆ LIVING

The 13 W̱SÁNEĆ moons marked the cycle of living for W̱SÁNEĆ Peoples for thousands of years prior to colonization. There were specific activities associated with each moon, and the W̱SÁNEĆ Peoples were busy throughout each entire cycle. Living and working in this way since time immemorial meant that we lived in harmony with our surroundings and passed on this knowledge through experiental embodied knowledge transfer from generation to generation.

> Our people lived as part of everything. We were so much a part of nature, we were just like the birds, the animals, the fish. We were just like the mountains. Our people lived that way.[100]

We were a part of the cycle of life in W̱SÁNEĆ lands, and this meant we had everything we needed and did not want for anything more. We lived in peace with our relatives and never forgot to give thanks for the gifts we received. Our lives did not follow the counting of years, but instead followed the cycle of the 13 W̱SÁNEĆ moons.

PEKELÁNEW—THE MOON THAT TURNS THE LEAVES WHITE. This moon signalled the end of the W̱SÁNEĆ SX̱OLE, as the last of our SĆÁÁNEW̱ relatives returned home to their spawning grounds. The W̱SÁNEĆ Peoples returned to their winter homes before the weather turned bad and travelling by canoe became too dangerous. The winds and seas became unpredictable for

100 Dave Elliot Sr., *Saltwater People: As told by Dave Elliot Sr.*, Saanich School District #63, 1983; Dave Elliot Sr., *Saltwater People.*

travel between our winter homes and the surrounding TETÁCES. The QOLEW̱ (Dog Salmon) were caught at what is now called Goldstream National Park.[101]

W̱ESELÁNEW̱—THE MOON OF THE SHAKER OF THE LEAVES. During the previous moon, the leaves changed colour, while during this moon, the leaves were shaken to the ground. Hunting parties are organized to go out hunting deer and elk. Ducks were caught at this time using two different types of net. The first type was hung between two fir trees over a bay or inlet, and the other was placed over the surface of the water. The ducks would fly into the former and fall to the ground, and in the latter the ducks would dive down and, in resurfacing, find themselves caught in the net. Final preparations were made in storing food and supplies for the coming winter. Winter fires were lit, and preparations were made for the coming winter dances.[102]

SJEL₡ÁSEṈ—THE MOON OF PUTTING YOUR PADDLE AWAY IN THE BUSH. Canoes and paddles were stored away for the winter owing to the dangerous sudden squalls and heavy rains making sea travel dangerous. Bad storms meant it was best to stay home, visit family and friends, and tell stories. Fishing took place in areas closer to the winter homes and clam digging was advantageous during low tide. There were many activities inside of the longhouses such as repairing any wear and tear on the SX̱OLE, carving, weaving, and creating tools. Preparations continued for the winter dances.[103]

SIS,ET—THE ELDER MOON. The days were short, and the storms were rough, so the W̱SÁNEĆ Peoples enjoyed the results of all the outdoor preparation, which allowed for us to stay safe and warm in our longhouses. This was the busiest time of year for our winter dances. The winter dances meant initiating new W̱SÁNEĆ

101 Earl Claxton and John Elliott, *The Saanich Year* (Saanich Indian School Board, 1993); Dave Elliot Sr., *Saltwater People.*

102 Claxton and Elliott, *The Saanich Year*; Dave Elliot Sr., *Saltwater People.*

103 Claxton and Elliott, *The Saanich Year*; Dave Elliot Sr., *Saltwater People.*

longhouse dancers, so this is around the time I would have been initiated as well. Dances were hosted in alternating longhouses, and when it was our turn, a feast and giveaways were prepared. The winter dances offered the best time for hearing stories and for passing on teachings to the younger dancers.[104]

N̲IN̲ENE—THE MOON OF THE CHILD. The days shifted and become longer, and the tides began to shift as well. The weather began to show signs of improving, and preparations began to increase for the next W̱SÁNEĆ SX̱OLE season. There was reparation and building of the nets and other materials used in the SX̱OLE. Halibut fishing was an option for those brave enough to hunt them. I recall my dad fishing halibut, and at the time those relatives far surpassed my slight five foot frame. The birth of deer fawns signalled the end of deer hunting. During the last several moons, ceremonial dances continued and so did the storytelling activities.[105] W̱SÁNEĆ Peoples could feel the beginnings of the warmer weather.

WEXES—THE MOON OF THE FROG. WEXES hold a special significance because they herald both the end of W̱SÁNEĆ longhouse ceremonial dances and the beginning of the new W̱SÁNEĆ season. When the W̱SÁNEĆ Peoples heard the WEXES they knew the weather would soon be warm and canoes were put back in the water because the weather became safer for making short trips. Herring returned to our territories and herring roe was gathered by placing a cedar branch in their spawning grounds and then collecting the branch and drying the roe in the sun and wind. It was a delicacy called QELEJ.[106] Spring salmon followed the herring and were also a delicacy at this time.

PEXSISEN̲—THE BLOSSOMING OUT MOON. During this moon, plant shoots were growing the first greens the W̱SÁNEĆ Peoples had had all winter. This was a good time of year to fell

104 Claxton and Elliott, *The Saanich Year*; Dave Elliot Sr., *Saltwater People.*
105 Claxton and Elliott, *The Saanich Year*; Dave Elliot Sr., *Saltwater People.*
106 Claxton and Elliott, *The Saanich Year*; Dave Elliot Sr., *Saltwater People.*

the large cedar trees, because the warming weather caused the sap to run, making it easier to strip the bark from the trees. The bark was saved and used later for making implements or weaving mats and clothing. During this time, wool was gathered from a breed of long-haired dog and goats that were shedding at that time of year. The wool was later spun and used for weaving blankets or other items. The blankets and other items were used in ceremony, including items specific to W̱SÁNEĆ longhouse winter dances. The dog breed has since gone extinct.[107]

SX̱ÁNEȽ—THE BULLHEAD MOON. Activities began to increase as the weather turned nicer and the W̱SÁNEĆ Peoples prepared to return to the summer camps. W̱SÁNEĆ Peoples began to spend more time on the water as the warm weather brings sudden thunder and lightning storms. Resources gathered included ȽEKES (seaweed), and SX̱ÁNEȽ (bullhead). The ȽEKES were gathered and spread out in the sun to dry. Once the ȽEKES were dry, they would be pressed together and stored away in blocks for the winter. During the cold winter months, they would be taken out to be used in cooking. To gather the SX̱ÁNEȽ, the W̱SÁNEĆ women and children would take woven cedar baskets down to the water and poke around boulders and rocks. The SX̱ÁNEȽ would make the noise "SḴÁ"—that is how it got its name. The SX̱ÁNEȽ arrived after a specific set of stars made its way across the sky and then disappeared beyond the horizon. This group of three stars was called PIOTEȽ (The Duck Hunters). A big wind arrived along with PIOTEȽ, and this heralded the arrival of SX̱ÁNEȽ.[108]

PENÁWEṈ—THE MOON OF THE CAMAS HARVEST. The days and evenings were warmer, and the rain was less frequent. W̱SÁNEĆ Peoples were now venturing to the TETÁCES as well as to the site where Stelly's High School now sits. In both places ḰȽO,EL (camas bulbs) were harvested, and in both locations, gulls also hatched their young, thereby fertilizing the ground that the

107 Claxton and Elliott, *The Saanich Year*; Dave Elliot Sr., *Saltwater People*.
108 Claxton and Elliott, *The Saanich Year*; Dave Elliot Sr., *Saltwater People*.

ḰȽO,EL grew in. Before Stelly's High School was built, the area was a marsh. It was drained, and thus ruined for camas and gull breeding grounds. The island ḰȽO,EL areas were ideal because they contained shallow topsoil over stone, creating nutrient-rich soil fertilized by the gulls. The W̱SÁNEĆ would only take eggs from a nest with more than one egg and less than four. If they took the only egg, the mother might abandon the nest. If they took from one with four, the mother would have been done laying eggs and be sitting on them, meaning they would be on their way to becoming chicks. Therefore, the W̱SÁNEĆ Peoples would take one egg if there were two, or two eggs if there were three. In the Elder tapes I was given access to while writing my *Arbutus Review* article in 2012, I recall one Elder speaking of the time his Elders saw the gulls eating the white man's garbage. The Elders said, "Those eggs will be no good no more."[109] Additional delicacies collected at this time of year included XIW̱E (purple sea urchins) and SQWIX̱I (green sea urchins)—a delicacy and a taste I never learned to acquire.[110]

ĆENŦEḴI—THE TIME OF THE SOCKEYE. By now, the days had grown longer and warmer, and the W̱SÁNEĆ Peoples had begun to move to summer camps. Preparation of nets, ropes and buoys had been completed, and these tools were ready for the upcoming SĆÁÁNEW̱ arrivals. The first of the salmon to arrive were the ŦEḴI ("sockeye" is an anglicized pronunciation of the Sencoten word ŦEḴI). Earl Claxton writes in *The Saanich Year*:

> The medicine man (ŚNÁEM) would paddle to the furthest point east and called on our ancient relative (the salmon) to come and feed the W̱SÁNEĆ people. He prayed, sang, and mentioned all the family reef net locations (SWÁLET) that the salmon would pass.[111]

109 Personal communication, Elder transcripts 2012.

110 Claxton and Elliott, *The Saanich Year*; Dave Elliot Sr., *Saltwater People.*

111 Claxton and Elliott, *The Saanich Year*, 13; Dave Elliot Sr., *Saltwater People.*

He also notes that:

> The Saanich People paid homage to the salmon with a very special song and ceremony to honor the salmon and show respect to its new generation. After the first sockeye salmon (known as the S,HIWEḰ leader) was caught, all fishing would cease and the ceremony of prayer and feast would begin.[112]

These ceremonies were vital to the relational, interrelated accountability we had to our SĆÁÁNEW̱ relatives. They were a way to show our appreciation to our SĆÁÁNEW̱ relatives, to our territories, and to TETÁCES and XÁLS themselves for the beautiful lives we had as W̱SÁNEĆ Peoples.[113]

In *Saltwater People*, Dave Elliot Sr. describes the ŦEḴI as "a pretty fish, with their beautiful green back, silver sides, plump shaped beautiful meat, bright red colour."[114] As a young boy, this researcher had the opportunity to fish with my dad and I had the experience of going out into our territories and pulling these beautiful SĆÁÁNEW̱ relatives from the sea—and that is a memory forever embedded in my mind. My dad is a contemporary commercial fisherman, and therefore we did not use the SX̱OLE. We were trawling instead, but I do remember the beautiful silver and green SĆÁÁNEW̱ with the dark red meat.

Throughout the next few moons, the W̱SÁNEĆ Peoples were very busy gathering additional resource items and attending and hosting longhouse gatherings. During these gatherings, the opportunity to share and trade the plentiful SĆÁÁNEW̱ occurred, and sharing what was plentiful for our people was another example of interrelated and relational accountability. This was the time of year both the inner bark of the willow tree and the bark of the SKELALNEW (cedar tree) were harvested and stored away, along

112 Claxton and Elliott, *The Saanich Year*, 13; Dave Elliot Sr., *Saltwater People.*

113 Claxton and Elliott, *The Saanich Year*; Dave Elliot Sr., *Saltwater People.*

114 Elliot Sr., *Salt Water People*, 48.

with the roots of the SKELALNEW. The inner bark of the willow tree was used for building and repairing the SX̲OLE, while the inner bark and roots of the SKELALNEW were used for weaving baskets and hats into intricate and incredibly precise works of art.[115]

ĆENHENEN—HUMPBACK SALMON RETURN TO THE EARTH. According to Dave Elliot Sr. in *Saltwater People*, these "were the most plentiful of all salmon" and he even recalls looking over the side of the canoe as a young boy and seeing "great schools passing under you. Thousands upon thousands of fish in one school."[116] When I fished with my dad, we never saw anything like that. In fact my dad would lament the fact that Japanese seiners would position themselves just outside of the international fishing boundary and throw out their huge nets to trap the fish and take them away. It is ironic that the government outlawed SX̲OLE and accused the W̱SÁNEĆ Peoples of using it to "trap" the SĆÁÁNEW̱—and there the Japanese were using a fishing system with nets so huge that few SĆÁÁNEW̱ were making it through (a literal trap).

This time of the year was referred to as ĆENQÁLES (time of heat) and was ideal because the SĆÁÁNEW̱ drying and storage became a W̱SÁNEĆ community activity. It took six people to work the SX̲OLE and two canoes. They would fill up each canoe and return to the beach to offload their catch. Those not participating with the SX̲OLE would be on the beach and help with cleaning and setting up the SĆÁÁNEW̱ to dry in the sun or smoked by the fire. During this time, we were also visiting our relatives who were working their own traditional SX̲OLE areas. This part of the year was busy and full of social activities.[117]

ĆENȽÁWEN—THE TIME OF THE COHO. The ȽÁWEN were caught, dried, and stored like the others. This time of year, the rains were increasing and the sun was getting farther away. This was a good time of year to catch rock cod and ling cod.[118] This practice

115 Claxton and Elliott, *The Saanich Year*; Dave Elliot Sr., *Saltwater People*.
116 Elliot Sr., *Salt Water People*, 50.
117 Claxton and Elliott, *The Saanich Year*; Dave Elliot Sr., *Saltwater People*.
118 Claxton and Elliott, *The Saanich Year*; Dave Elliot Sr., *Saltwater People*.

was a favorite of mine because my Dad would anchor the boat near one of the rocky areas near one of our TETÁCES. Individual fishing lines were then thrown off the side of the boat and we would "jig" for cod. I liked it and caught many. One time I even managed to "jig" a ling cod. At the time I was too young to pull up this aggressive fish, so my older brother had to bring it in for me. But we had battered fish and chips that night that I caught myself. That is a good memory.

This brings the W̱SÁNEĆ seasonal cycle and the 13 W̱SÁNEĆ moons back around to where we started. This is by no means meant to be an exhaustive list of the activities conducted by my people over the course of one seasonal cycle. It is only meant to demonstrate some of the pre-colonization seasonal cycle activities, so that I may then move on to discuss the ways that we have lost these practices and the effects this loss has had on W̱SÁNEĆ Peoples. Embodied W̱SÁNEĆ Knowledge transfer in the traditional manner is impossible today, and my research seeks to explore alternative methods of embodied W̱SÁNEĆ Knowledge transfer utilizing theatre and performance studies. I would like to reiterate my gratitude and give thanks to the three main sources for this section: Dave Elliot Sr.'s *The Saltwater People* (1983), *ÁLENENEC: Learning From Homeland* (2008) by W̱SÁNEĆ Community members and the Saanich Adult Education Centre, and *The Saanich Year* (1993) by Earl Claxton and John Elliott. Additional thanks are due for Dr. Nicholas Xemtoltw Claxton's exemplary MA and PhD dissertation research in 2008 and 2015 at the University of Victoria.

CONTEMPORARY EMBODIED W̱SÁNEĆ KNOWLEDGE TRANSFER

W̱SÁNEĆ ceremonial longhouse dances are the one practice that has continued uninterrupted since time immemorial. The potlatch bans from 1884 to 1951 affected our longhouse practices because they necessitated that those practices go underground, conducted in remote locations in secret. Additionally, this caused the practices to continue without the ability to travel between nations easily, and resulted in some of the practices becoming lost or altered from one Indigenous nation to the next. There is a resurgence of W̱SÁNEĆ longhouse dancing occurring, and it is a testament to desire for the collective return to this vital and important embodied practice. I believe it is imperative that we nurture the one practice we have kept, while we strive to reacquire as many as we can of those articulated in this chapter that have been lost.

Unfortunately for the W̱SÁNEĆ Peoples, we lost many of the activities listed in this chapter. The Oregon Treaty of 1846 established the imaginary line between Canada and the United States and cut off W̱SÁNEĆ access to many traditional SX̱OLE areas we had maintained and used since time immemorial. The Douglas Treaty the W̱SÁNEĆ signed in 1852 dictated that we could hunt and fish as before, but did not define our traditional hunting or fishing areas. It included only the land mass now called the Saanich Peninsula, and did not include our TETÁCES or areas we used around what is now called Goldstream National Park. Eventually, our TETÁCES were sold. Most of the remaining traditional W̱SÁNEĆ territories have been developed and are now crowded with houses and businesses, and divided into municipalities. Development has destroyed plants, wildlife, and the ecology that supported them. Many of the practices outlined in this chapter are not possible within W̱SÁNEĆ territories anymore.

Dr. Nicholas Xemtoltw Claxton's PhD dissertation articulates his journey of how he successfully brought the SX̱OLE back to the W̱SÁNEĆ Peoples. It was done in an accessible way by bringing traditional embodied teachings to the students at the W̱SÁNEĆ tribal school - ȽÁU, WELṈEW̱. The students were allowed to participate in the making of different parts of the SX̱OLE and they were also given the teachings from Elders at the same time. Models of what would eventually become the full-scale working SX̱OLE are on display at W̱SÁNEĆ tribal school - ȽÁU, WELṈEW̱.

ȽÁU, WELṈEW̱ tribal school does a great job of balancing western education practices with W̱SÁNEĆ Knowledge, but it can only do so much. ȽÁU, WELṈEW̱ offers Sencoten language lessons with W̱SÁNEĆ Elders in addition to field trips the W̱SÁNEĆ lands. However, with the loss of so much of the land base and access to our TETÁCES so limited, a true embodied experience is not possible. What other options are available for the W̱SÁNEĆ Peoples to connect with traditional practices that would be consistent with embodied W̱SÁNEĆ Knowledge transfer? My research seeks to explore how I, as a W̱SÁNEĆ artist and academic, draw on embodied W̱SÁNEĆ Knowledge in my artistic and academic work. Performance studies and knowledge of how to utilize the performativity of traditional embodied W̱SÁNEĆ Knowledge transfer, in addition to Spiderwoman Theater, Gloria Miguel, and Storyweaving performance methodology, together offer the basis for my concept of contemporary W̱SÁNEĆ Knowledge transfer.

SX̱ I¸ÁM

(STORYTIME)

ṈOS

(FOUR)

SȻI¸NONET[1]

Frank was lost and walking through a white mist. He could feel the earth beneath his feet. Were those moccasins on his feet? He squinted his eyes as he tried to make out something to tell him where he was. Then maybe he could figure out why he was there. Suddenly the mist began to evaporate and lose its thick feel and he began to make out small mounds stretching far off in the distance. He noticed there were men and women standing on the mounds, one person for each of the mounds, as far as the eye could see. They were all speaking at once, but all Frank could hear was a cacophony of whispers resulting in a white noise. Frank noticed that every single one of them was facing the same direction, and as he turned to look to his left, he realized the sun was rising in the direction the people were praying to.

Frank knew they were greeting the new day and welcoming a new beginning. When he turned back, he saw they were all clasping both hands to their chests. They slowly extended both arms forward, with the left hand over the right. In each of their left hands Frank saw they held a small item, and he instinctively knew it was their gift—their SȻI¸NONET. Frank saw all of those W̱SÁNEĆ relatives, and it made him happy, and he began to laugh. Soon, the laughter turned to tears as he watched his ancestors holding their very souls out to the coming day, to the new beginning, and to the prospect of a fresh start. Frank began to sob as the meaning hit home.

They were communicating to him that he should do the same...

1 Spiritual Power

I, A W̱SÁNEĆ ARTIST AND ACADEMIC

W̱SÁNEĆ PLACES AND SPACES

There is something interesting happening in the archive-obsessed world of western science. They are discovering more and more archivable evidence of Indigenous "existence" in North America. Recently, in White Sands National Park in New Mexico, there has been a discovery of fossil footprints indicating human habitation between 21,000 and 23,000 years ago.[2] This is several thousand years earlier than the last archival data indicated. Of course, Indigenous oral history has always shown our existence to pre-date this new finding, but because our oral history is not quantifiable or archivable, we wait until the next "find" the scientists make. W̱SÁNEĆ oral history tells me we were placed here *before* they created the mountains.

Our northern neighbours in the Queen Charlotte Islands discovered the bones of a massive ancient grizzly bear and a spear point

2 Tom Metcalfe, "Fossil footprints show humans in North America more than 21,000 years ago," NBCNews.com, September 23, 2021. Retrieved March 28, 2022, from https://www.nbcnews.com/science/science-news/fossil-footprints-show-humans-north-america-21000-years-ago-rcna2169.

dating back to 11,000 years ago.[3] A Heiltsuk village site dates back 13,600 to 14,000 years ago, making that site three times as old as the Great Pyramid at Giza.[4] In W̱SÁNEĆ territory, SḴŦAḴ (Mayne Island) once held a stone bowl estimate to be 4,000 to 6,000 years old—until someone came along and stole it from us. According to the accepted archivable data set, this means our existence in W̱SÁNEĆ territories dates back at least as long as those inhabitants around the Great Pyramid at Giza. Except there is a reason our oral history tells us we were placed at SṈIDȻEȽ *before* the mountains were created by XÁLS. It is because we have always been here, since time immemorial.

The reason I had to rely so heavily on aforementioned texts *The Saltwater People*, *ÁLENENEC: Learning From Homeland*, and *The Saanich Year*, is because W̱SÁNEĆ Knowledge transfer is traditionally done through in-person, experiential teaching and learning. There are not many written accounts of traditional W̱SÁNEĆ Knowledge available. There are some incredible initiatives happening within W̱SÁNEĆ territories, such as Dr. Nicholas Xemtoltw Claxton's project to return SX̱OLE to the W̱SÁNEĆ. There have also been canoe journeys that permit W̱SÁNEĆ students to travel through our traditional hunting and gathering places. I know people still gather cedar bark and roots for weaving, and that our longhouse winter dances are going strong. However, it is undeniable that most of the traditional practices described in the three W̱SÁNEĆ books are no longer possible. The resources are gone or diminished, and our access to traditional lands and seas no longer exists. There are many incredible W̱SÁNEĆ educators working to make sure this

3 Devon Bidal, "Archaeologists have unearthed exciting secrets on Haida Gwaii," *Hakai Magazine*, December 9, 2021. Retrieved March 28, 2022, from https://hakaimagazine.com/news/haida-gwaiis-caves-have-been-hiding-a-huge-secret/.

4 Randy Shore, "Heiltsuk First Nation Village among oldest in North America: Archeologists," *Vancouver Sun* March 29, 2017. Retrieved March 28, 2022, from https://vancouversun.com/news/local-news/heiltsuk-first-nation-village-among-oldest-in-north-america-archeologists.

knowledge remains alive, and this is where research exploring embodied W̱SÁNEĆ Knowledge transfer and the praxis of theatre and performance studies becomes significant.

Recall Victor Turner and Richard Schechner, two of the founders of performance studies theory. Their earlier work explores the praxis of traditional ritual in non-western cultures and theatre and/or performance. According to Schechner, anything that represents *twice-behaved* behaviour could be considered a performance. If we take this concept in conjunction with Diana Taylor's "so-called ephemeral *repertoire* of embodied practice/knowledge (i.e., spoken language, dance, sports, ritual)," we get an idea of the potential in the meeting of performance studies theory and embodied practice/knowledge.[5] There is something uniquely important in research that explores the possibility of maintaining embodied knowledge outside of written text. I repeat an earlier statement: Embodied Indigenous Knowledge is malleable and adaptable to parallel the adaptability of our peoples, and so the knowledge can be contemporary although it may have originated a millennium ago. How I, as a W̱SÁNEĆ artist and academic, envision and employ this working concept has resulted in this dissertation research.

W̱SÁNEĆ Peoples cannot go back to pre-contact times because those places and spaces no longer exist, and we have not had to access those embodied skills for a very long time. However, this does not mean that we cannot still attempt to access and practice them. If anything, recent global events are a warning that this is exactly what we should be doing. We may not have access to the resources and the land base, but we still have access to embodied W̱SÁNEĆ Knowledge and to the means to make it happen. Embodied W̱SÁNEĆ Knowledge transfer using the ephemeral repertoire of twice-behaved behaviour offers one way to accomplish this task. Traditional teaching involved demonstrating by doing, while traditional learning involved watching and doing. This behaviour, then, would fall under what Schechner referred to

5 Taylor, *The Archive and the Repertoire*,19.

as twice-behaved behaviour—our traditional embodied W̱SÁNEĆ Knowledge transfer was once very performative in that sense. In W̱SÁNEĆ reality, this was the key to traditional teaching and learning, which was itself key to W̱SÁNEĆ living.

MURIEL MIGUEL AND STORYWEAVING PERFORMANCE METHODOLOGY

In 2015, as a part of Trent University's Indigenous Studies PhD program, I was tasked with securing a practicum placement with an Indigenous organization. Ideally, the organization chosen would be related to my research area. I was fortunate to locate a practicum position with the Centre for Indigenous Theatre summer intensive. The Centre for Indigenous Theatre is a three-year theatre program for Indigenous youth located in Toronto, Ontario. I secured a practicum placement as the assistant to the stage manager, but after a few days, the executive director of the program, Rose Stella, and the main director of the theatre intensive, Muriel Miguel, thought I would get a better feel for the program if I were to take part in the process. I was reluctant because I had not engaged with this type of intensive physical theatre work in decades, but in retrospect, they were of course correct.

Muriel Miguel was, and continues to be the artistic director and one of the founding members of Spiderwoman Theater, the longest running Indigenous-women's theatre company in the world. Through her, I was introduced to the Storyweaving performance methodology in July of 2015, and I immediately realized how valuable it would be for demonstrating contemporary traditional embodied W̱SÁNEĆ Knowledge. The Storyweaving performance methodology created and developed by Muriel Miguel and Spiderwoman Theater has been workshopped and taught around the world in a process described on their website, in which participants are invited to:

> Investigate the unique process that the women of Spiderwoman Theater use to create their plays. "Storyweaving" describes the layering of stories, images, sound, movement and music, creating a three-dimensional tapestry which is embodied in space and becomes the theatre production. Incorporating the exercises that have been learned in the workshop, the participants will collectively build a performance of the stories which they will then present (Spiderwoman Theatre, n.d.).

It is understandable that the Storyweaving performance methodology is congruent with traditional embodied Indigenous Knowledge because of the deep connection Muriel Miguel and her sisters have with their Indigenous ancestry. Each of the Miguel sisters was trained in non-indigenous theater methods by prestigious acting teachers such as Uta Hagen, Joseph Chaikin, and Lee Strasberg.[6] Through the founding and development of Spiderwoman Theater, the sisters began to connect with their Indigenous roots as they developed the Storyweaving performance methodology.

Spiderwoman Theater "takes its name from the Hopi goddess Spiderwoman, who taught the people to weave and said, 'There must be a flaw in every tapestry so that my sprit may come and go at will'."[7] It is significant how the longer quote above highlights how Storyweaving creates "a three-dimensional tapestry which is embodied in space" in direct correlation to my proposed research and to the subsequent artistic vision of Muriel Miguel. Monique Mojica and Ric Knowles write about Spiderwoman Theater's work

6 Larry Abbott "Spiderwoman Theatre and the Tapestry of Story," *Canadian Journal of Native Studies* XVI, 1 (1996): 165–180; Ross Kidd, "Reclaiming Culture: Indigenous Performers Take Back Their Show," *The Canadian Journal Of Native Studies* 4, 1 (1984): 105–120.

7 Ric Knowles and Monique Mojica, eds., "Introduction," in *Staging Coyote's Dream: An Anthology of First Nations Drama in English* (Toronto: Playwrights Canada Press: 2003), iii-vii.

in terms reminiscent of the concept of Diana Taylor's ephemeral embodied knowledge:

> Their work is often difficult to follow on the page, but when performed it comes fully to life as physical, embodied, and emotional connections are woven together seamlessly and with considerable theatrical nuance.[8]

Embodiment is a consistent theme in the Storyweaving performance methodology, and it is for this reason that the process of creating W̱SÁNEĆ ȾÁLE: TOWARD A W̱SÁNEĆ KNOWLEDGE, in conjunction with the Storyweaving performance methodology, will demonstrate how traditional W̱SÁNEĆ Knowledge can be both contemporary and have existed since time immemorial. Here I demonstrate how I, as a W̱SÁNEĆ artist and academic, am forever connected to the history of W̱SÁNEĆ people through ephemeral and embodied practices passed down from my W̱SÁNEĆ ancestors. Traditional W̱SÁNEĆ Knowledge continues to exist *because* it has been passed down in embodied ephemeral formats since time immemorial.

The Centre for Indigenous Theatre summer theatre intensive was incredible, and I cannot say enough about what a gift it is for the youth who attend. The days began with either movement or voice as a warmup. Before lunch, the director, Muriel Miguel, would conduct theatre exercises to familiarize the students with her acting process. After lunch, Miguel conducted work more focused on each participant's personal stories. A healthy dinner was also provided, after which there were a variety of activities such as Indigenous song work, making individual rattles, and the construction of t-shirts of individual design, which would eventually become our show costumes. At the end of each week, there was a circle check-in where everyone was encouraged to share their thoughts,

8 Knowles and Mojica, "Introduction," 100.

feelings, and experiences from the past week. A table was set up in the theatre with smudge materials made available from day one, which people had access to and could use at any time during the workshop. Because of the nature of the work, the smudging table was used often, as the Storyweaving process challenged all of the participants mentally, emotionally, physically, and spiritually.

The program was set up to include Indigenous Knowledge from guest lecturers invited to speak over the course of the summer session. The program began with a trip to the Petroglyphs, on which Elder Merritt Taylor spoke and then led a circle to allow the students to share their impressions. The students were very moved by their visit, so much so that when choosing the name of the show they, decided on "Enji Bwaajigaadeg Siniing," which means "Dreams from the Stones." Elder Shirley Williams spoke and shared her teachings about water and the water walks. Leanne Betasamosake Simpson also spoke and shared her artistic work involving spoken word and music, along with her process for creating those pieces. Elder Merritt Taylor conducted a sweat at the request of the students. The Indigenous youth were therefore exposed to different types of Indigenous Knowledge from Elders, Indigenous artists, and Indigenous academics.

The movement and voice portions of the program combined with the theatre exercises provided by Miguel were designed to work on several levels. The program design was meant to familiarize the students with the basic building blocks of common theatre practices. Next, the goals were to familiarize the students with each other and with the staff, many of whom had never met before this program. The intention was to build group cohesion and create an ensemble. Finally, as instructors, we were expected to lead by example and show the students how to fearlessly tackle each exercise, so they could see that this was a safe space for them to do the same. Throughout this process, the students were developing two personal stories, each of which Miguel then developed in the Spiderwoman Storyweaving fashion. Miguel then organized the stories in a specific order to present as our final show. The week before the shows, we worked extremely long days, and there was much exhaustion all around. I kept a journal during the whole process and did my best to write in it every day. When I read it back, it would seem the main theme was the physical exhaustion and how the physicality of this type of work caused some minor injuries.

I must give big heartfelt thanks to Artistic Director of CIT, Rose Stella, and to Muriel Miguel for encouraging me to become a part of the process. It was invaluable for me to experience the work from the inside, and therefore to be able to watch the students as they worked through the program. Most of the students had never been on stage before or even in an acting class, so their growth from day one to the performance was staggering to witness. I particularly enjoyed watching for the moment when the students suddenly "got" what the director wanted. It was this incredible flash of understanding, after which their work invariably became more focused and expansive. From that point the Storyweaving really began to take shape. Miguel expected everyone to develop and practice individual stories to share. As the workshop progressed, we began to share our stories with the group and did our best to incorporate as many of the lessons from the previous classes, including voice work and movement, as we could. It was expected that we incorporate the teachings and avoid just standing in one place and telling our stories—therefore our stories eventually included a great deal of movement and vocal dynamics. During this process, Muriel challenged us, and often coaxed the most amazing performances out of us.

I began with the purpose of working as the assistant to the stage manager and ended up becoming a participant in the CIT program. Then, at the end of the second week, the man who had been hired to be the movement/choreographer had to drop out for medical reasons. Because CIT knew I had a background in dance, I was asked to step into the role of movement/choreography director. This meant I would assume the responsibility of leading daily physical warmup/conditioning exercises, as well as working with the existing choreography to make sure everyone was in sync. I was tasked with choreographing whatever Muriel Miguel needed that had not been completed by the previous movement director. The piece that I worked on that became my favourite was "The Chair Dance" with a young man who was a double amputee. The Indigenous youth had lost his right arm and right leg in a train accident, and during the program he wrote a rap song about it. He was working in a chair with wheels and Miguel thought it might be interesting if I choreographed a number with him and the chair. So prior to his rap song, we had him come on stage and dance to *Brandenburg Concerto no. 3*. It was the Indigenous youth's moment to shine, and he loved the number. For me, it was great to contribute to their healing, learning, and growth.

I realized during the second week of the program that Miguel's work was a perfect example of the subject of my academic research. I became interested in exploring how contemporary Indigenous artists and academics use embodied Indigenous Knowledge in their artistic and academic pursuits. I wanted to explore how stories, songs, dances, and traditional activities (anything not text-based) are explored and drawn from that embodied space in to contemporary academic and artistic work. Through CIT and Muriel Miguel, the students in the program were taking their own stories and bringing them to life through storytelling, dance, song, and Indigenous Knowledge teachings. What made the show so special for me was knowing most of the students had never been on stage, and that for many, this was the first time they were allowed to tell their own stories in a public forum—a forum where people listened, applauded their work, and gave them positive feedback after the show. It was an empowering experience. I knew this experience had the potential to benefit my research by allowing me to explore Muriel's process as well as to test my research by using my own embodied W̱SÁNEĆ Knowledge.

The CIT program did not attempt to intellectualize embodied Indigenous Knowledge—they simply did it.[9] The work CIT does incorporates song, dance, storytelling and connections to land and place to create embodied knowledge with Indigenous youth. I believe this to be the main reason the program is so successful, and why it is such a powerful and transformative experience for all involved. I saw immediately how important this work was from an Indigenous perspective. None of it was written down and all of it came from the Indigenous youth themselves. They made connections to their pasts, to their families, and to their communities and/or nations. It was humbling and illustrated the power that the ephemeral repertoire can have. I made note of this experience and I knew it would become a part of my research. In summer of 2015, I wrote a monologue that I titled *The Picnic*. Without realizing it, I had created my first rudimentary example of embodied W̱SÁNEĆ Knowledge. A written transcript of that performance precedes this chapter.

While it is not possible to embody W̱SÁNEĆ Knowledge the way that my ancestors did, I believe that integrating the Storyweaving performance methodology with traditional W̱SÁNEĆ Knowledge practices yields promising results. By Storyweaving embodied W̱SÁNEĆ Knowledge, I engaged viewers in an embodied practice utilizing sound and movement knowledge transfer in the way my ancestors did, through doing and showing, while the participants/viewers were engaging in more traditional learning in the form of watching and doing. This contemporary model of embodied W̱SÁNEĆ Knowledge transfer is of course not an exact replica of traditional embodied W̱SÁNEĆ Knowledge transfer, which I

9 During my defense, dissertation committee member Monique Mojica questioned my use of "intellectualize" and thought it implied CIT and Indigenous theatre in general was not an intellectual practice. I meant that CIT and embodied Indigenous Knowledge was holistic and encompassed the intellectual, spiritual, emotional, and physical. It did not simply engage "from the neck up" in the way that academia does.

have already established is no longer possible in the contemporary W̱SÁNEĆ world.

In the next section, I deconstruct the monologue *The Picnic* that I created and performed at the 2015 CIT summer theatre intensive under the direction of Muriel Miguel. At the time I created it, I was simply developing and performing a monologue using the Storyweaving performance methodology. However, now that I am aware of the applicability of the Storyweaving process to embodied W̱SÁNEĆ Knowledge transfer, I can deconstruct the monologue and offer ways that I can improve it. The proposed improvements are meant to enhance the teaching and learning experience and to facilitate an increase of embodied W̱SÁNEĆ Knowledge transfer.

THE PICNIC AS EMBODIED W̱SÁNEĆ KNOWLEDGE TRANSFER

When I agreed that taking part in the theatre intensive was the best way to engage with the process, I knew what I was getting myself into. It had been decades since I had been involved in this type of work, and this was my first time working with Muriel Miguel and the Storyweaving performance methodology. This type of work requires a fearlessness and honesty that is exciting and terrifying in equal measure. It must be done openly and honestly, or it doesn't work. The workshop participants were required to keep journals while at the intensive and to record our thoughts on the work and any interesting stories or dreams we had during that time. The stories could be about our childhood, fond or disturbing memories, family history, or stories from our Indigenous nations. I had just returned from W̱SÁNEĆ territories and visiting family. While there, I took the opportunity to gather stories as well. During a visit with one of my sisters, she pulled out a photo album with some old pictures I had not viewed before. One of the pictures was of a family picnic we had on one of our TETÁCES. It was an activity we did periodically, and it involved taking Dad's boat out. It is one of the few cherished memories I have. The picture is of me and my sister sitting on a big rock formation on the beach. I remembered the day vividly, and while I was journaling for CIT, the entire story came out on the page.

The beauty of the Storyweaving process for me was that it was not about acting out a monologue or reciting words from a script—it was about reliving a story or creating/recreating an experience. Once the students became accustomed to working together and periodically performing small exercises in front of one another, we started to share our stories. This usually happened at the end of the day when we were relaxed and/or tired and our defenses were down (or at least lowered). Muriel would point to people and ask them to tell a story. We did not stand up with a script in hand. Nor did we stand still and recite memorized lines. We shared a story and included sound and movement—our embodied memories were reenacted so that the other students could share in a collective experience. Traditional Indigenous storytelling has always involved the viewers in the process.

I do not remember much of what I said or did the first time I stood up and shared this story. I started with "There was this picture. And it reminded me of a story." As soon as I spoke the words, I could see the picture in my hand, and I could feel my mind transported back to that giant rock on the beach. I was transported back and every part of the story that came next was fully remembered in an embodied story sharing experience. It was cathartic. After the first telling, the Storyweaving process requires repetition of a piece over and over until the body remembers it in this new setting and format. The piece gradually becomes a shared, embodied storytelling experience.

When I examine *The Picnic* now, I can see that it was never meant to represent embodied W̱SÁNEĆ Knowledge transfer. It was created to share a story that was representative of early life for me as a W̱SÁNEĆ boy, to explain a little bit about W̱SÁNEĆ territories, and to touch on the death of my late mom. In this story, I illustrate an important connection between myself and my younger sister (she was four and I was five), and after one of our performances an Indigenous man said it reminded him of his own relationship with his sister. That is one example of the ability this type of work can have to make connections. Only now, years later, can I see the potential in recreating *The Picnic* with the intent of using it for embodied W̱SÁNEĆ Knowledge transfer. It is ideal to directly engage the audience and to involved them in the process. In 2015, I was new to the Storyweaving process and therefore engaging the audience in my storytelling would not have occurred to me.

When considering *The Picnic* now, with the benefit of hindsight and all the research I have conducted about embodied W̱SÁNEĆ Knowledge transfer, I can see there are three distinct places in the story in which I could have easily added embodied W̱SÁNEĆ Knowledge. The first is at the beginning of story, after the introduction of my family and the boat journey itself. This would be the perfect place for and introduction of how the W̱SÁNEĆ Peoples came to be. Here I would insert the story of how the first W̱SÁNEĆ person was placed down on the ancient village site of SN̲IDȻEŁ, and how XÁLS created the surrounding mountains, including ŁÁU, WELN̲EW̱ and PKOLS, and then took the W̱SÁNEĆ Peoples up PKOLS and threw some of our W̱SÁNEĆ relatives out into the surrounding waters. This is how they became our TETÁCES—relatives of the deep.

The second opportunity for embodied W̱SÁNEĆ Knowledge transfer would be during the story of our encounter with the KELŁOLEMEĆEN (Killer Whale). I do briefly mention the story during the monologue, but it would be a great opportunity to really elaborate on it. In the traditional story, the SW̱EW̱O,EȾ (Thunderbird) lives in a cave on ŁÁU, WELN̲EW̱. There is a monster of a KELŁOLEMEĆEN who is eating all the SĆÁÁNEW̱, and the W̱SÁNEĆ Peoples are beginning to starve. The W̱SÁNEĆ Peoples pray to XÁLS for help, and he sends the SW̱EW̱O,EȾ. SW̱EW̱O,EȾ dives down and picks up the KELŁOLEMEĆEN in their talons, and they fly high up into the sky. It is an epic battle in which the clash of the two beings causes lightning, and when the SW̱EW̱O,EŦ drops the KELŁOLEMEĆEN, the sound of thunder is heard when KELŁOLEMEĆEN hits the water.[10]

The third place I envision implementing embodied W̱SÁNEĆ Knowledge transfer is after the boy and his sister reach the top of the mountain. This would be an ideal spot to insert the story that is included in the SX̱I,ÁM (Storytime) sections NEȻE (One) and ŁIW̱ (Three). In this story, SWÍ,ḴE (Wife) becomes SYÁ,TEN (Widow) and embarks on a journey in which she establishes the W̱SÁNEĆ village area of W̱JOŁEŁP—"The place of maples." It is a beautiful story that affirms the strength of W̱SÁNEĆ women and explains how the story of W̱JOŁEŁP began on one of our TETÁCES. W̱SÁNEĆ language, W̱SÁNEĆ history, W̱SÁNEĆ resource gathering practices, and more would be demonstrated using the Storyweaving performance methodology as a contemporary teaching and learning tool. Twice-behaved behaviour through contemporary W̱SÁNEĆ Knowledge transfer in an engaging and entertaining format.

The Picnic as it stands now is a monologue in which some aspects of W̱SÁNEĆ Knowledge are conveyed to the audience. However, by engaging with the concept of embodied W̱SÁNEĆ Knowledge transfer and inserting the three previous story ideas, I could change the piece from a storytelling monologue to an experiential learning event. Those engaging in the embodied W̱SÁNEĆ Knowledge transfer experience would learn SENĆOŦEN words as well as some of the important history of our Peoples and territories. Additionally, they would learn of the connection we have as W̱SÁNEĆ Peoples to our territory and get a sense of how long we have existed there. For W̱SÁNEĆ participants, this would offer a sense of pride, place, and community. All of this would be done in a way that was more in line with traditional forms of W̱SÁNEĆ teaching and learning.

10 W̱SÁNEĆ Community members, Saanich Adult Education Centre et al, *ÁLENENEC*, 2008.

W̱SÁNEĆ FIRST, W̱SÁNEĆ ARTIST SECOND, AND ACADEMIC THIRD

My writing and research have now come full circle. The prologue of this book contains two pictures from my childhood, and both are of me and my family doing what the W̱SÁNEĆ Peoples have done since time immemorial—we are out on the water visiting our TETÁCES. Now almost fifty years later I am remembering, writing, and performing contemporary embodied W̱SÁNEĆ Knowledge. I feel a sense of pride and know that I am privileged to have embodied many of the traditional W̱SÁNEĆ Knowledges. I am also saddened and worried that today's W̱SÁNEĆ youth lack the opportunities that I've had. The world is on fire and W̱SÁNEĆ children, youth, and families are being drowned in the noise of digital media—in platforms designed to work from the neck up. This book represents a small part of a much bigger project. By moving away from the standard one-dimensional social sciences research process, I have come full circle and found research that is truly and authentically embodied W̱SÁNEĆ Knowledge. The following section articulates the embodied W̱SÁNEĆ Knowledge transfer project titled *The Picnic* in an expanded and completed format.

I hear the WEXES—which means I have come full circle to where it began.

SX̱ I¸ÁM

(STORYTIME)

L̄ḴÁĆES

(FIVE)

ȻL̄ĆELÁL I ESEBT ES[11]

SX̱I¸ÁM (ONE FINAL STORYTIME)

Frank stared at the laptop screen as he contemplated his next steps. He felt like the widow SYÁ¸TEN at the end of her long journey as she walked through the forest of maple trees to discover the beauty that would eventually become W̱JOȽEȽP. W̱JOȽEȽP was where Frank had spent the first three years of his life, and it was the birthplace of his mom, his grandmother, and his ancestor Chowithet—Frank's namesake and a signatory to the Douglas treaty. Frank felt he was the anti-hero in this journey, and he was fine with that. Imperfections are what make us interesting, and only through trial and error do we discover the path our lives are meant to take.

Frank knew that in the end he would produce something unique to his journey. He decided early on that it would be far removed from the expected research format, and that it was going to be special to him. It would house all the pain and growth. It would be honest and upfront. And it would unequivocally contain his truth. Tying up the loose ends as much as possible is important in order to offer a sense of closure and to recognize the end of the cycle; to herald the beginning of something new. Life comes in cycles, and Frank knew that it was time to close this chapter for good.

11 English translation: They have almost completed it.

Frank's journey is represented throughout W̱SÁNEĆ ȾÁLE: TOWARD A W̱SÁNEĆ KNOWLEDGE. Just as he is the young boy pictured in the prologue who eventually visits his TETÁCES island relatives, or that guy who wakes up in detox and contemplates the paved city streets below—saddened by the knowledge that it was once pristine wilderness inhabited by his ancestors, Frank is the guy who survived the university experience. He is the guy who keeps hearing similar stories from Indigenous academics in other institutions. The ancestors were there with Frank on the ocean, they were there when he ran up ŁÁU WELṈEW̱ to bathe in the stream, and when he did the same in the Salish Sea. The ancestors were there when he was presented to the community as a traditional W̱SÁNEĆ dancer and then they returned to him at a crucial point in the dream that gave him strength to keep going in the face of adversity.

Frank felt that he was finally able to move on in his life. He was healing, ready to forgive, and ready to reconcile the whole affair. Frank knew there was one final SX̱I¸ÁM to tell to bring his story full circle. How would he, a WSANEC artist and academic, utilize embodied WSANEC knowledge in his artistic and academic work? He knew exactly how this writing would end—in the way that it had begun—with a picture. Frank sat down at his laptop and began typing.

"There was this picture...and it reminded me of a story..."

THE PICNIC[12]

There was this picture

And it reminded me of this story

When I was really little, my dad used to take us out on his fishing boat

We used to go out on picnics in the surrounding islands in our territory

NEȾE (One) SX̱I,ÁM!!

Interspersed throughout this performance are SX̱I,ÁM (Stories) about the W̱SÁNEĆ Nation. The SX̱I,ÁM are designed to introduce you to W̱SÁNEĆ stories, places, and spaces. NEȾE means ONE. Everyone together NEȾE—ONE!

NEȾE (One) SX̱I,ÁM (Story) is about W̱SÁNEĆ places.

XÁLS (Creator) gave the W̱SÁNEĆ a beautiful place to live, and we had an abundance of everything we needed. XÁLS placed the first W̱SÁNEĆ person down in what would become the most ancient of W̱SÁNEĆ village sites, called SṈIDȻEŁ. SṈIDȻEŁ means "place of blue grouse" because they were once plentiful in that area. SṈIDȻEŁ was stolen from the W̱SÁNEĆ Peoples.

12 Jack Horne, *The Picnic*. https://youtu.be/z9CSjqP_84U.

It is the area around what is now called the Todd Inlet and includes the world-famous tourist attraction called the Butchart Gardens. SLEMEW̱ (Rain) was the first W̱SÁNEĆ person placed down at SṈIDȻEȽ, and there the W̱SÁNEĆ Peoples learned to live in harmony with their relatives like the SMÍEŦ (deer) and SĆÁÁNEW̱ (Salmon). These were some of the relatives to the W̱SÁNEĆ Peoples, and we all lived in harmony and took care of one another.

Returning to The Picnic...

So we'd load up our entire family onto his boat and we'd head out onto the sea

Because I was really little

my sister was four and I was five

we had to sit in the cabin with our dad together

She got to sit on his lap

And I had to stand on top of this really tall stool and we'd both be staring out the window

And our job was to watch for logs that were submerged under the water to make sure that we didn't crash!

So we're travelin' along

Lookin' for our logs

And after a REALLY long time, we finally make it to the island

So my dad stops the engine

He sneaks along the side of the boat so he can get the anchor

And I always freak out that he's going to fall over

And he picks up this giant anchor, and he chucks it over!

SPLOOSH!!

And then he makes his way to the back of the boat

And then he pulls in this rowboat

He pulls in the rowboat, gets it along side

And loads on the first group of people that are headed to shore

They all get in

And my dad sits there and he rows... and he rows... and he rows...

Now the big kids got to go first because they all had jobs to do

They had to get firewood, look for crabs, look for clams

Whatever else they needed to do

But because my sister was four, and I was five

We had to sit on the boat and wait alone together

And after a VERY long time, my Dad finally makes it back to the boat

And it's our turn

So he lifts us onto the rowboat, one at a time

First me, and then my sister

There are TWO rules in the rowboat

You have to SIT STILL

And you have to HOLD HANDS

And that's it

So we head to shore

And my dad's rowing... and my dad's rowing... and my dad's rowing?

And then I can see the people on the shore

And they're kinda freakin' out a little

They're saying, "HEY! HURRY UP!"

And my dad's rowing

And they're freaking out

They're saying, "HEY! YOU BETTER HURRY UP!"

So my dad stops rowing and we all look over and...

All of a sudden there's this...this family, this whole family of KELŁOLEMEĆEN[13]

And they're just sailing their ways through the water

And we get so excited, my sister and I, because it reminds us of the story of the Thunderbird, and the KELŁOLEMEĆEN

ĆESE (Two) SX̲I,ÁM!!
Everyone together - ĆESE (Two) SX̲I,ÁM (Story)

A long time ago, the W̱SÁNEĆ People were starving because a great KELŁOLEMEĆEN (Whale) was eating all of the salmon. The Thunderbird was a benevolent being who felt sorry for the W̱SÁNEĆ People and decided to help them. The Thunderbird flew out over the water until he spotted the KELŁOLEMEĆEN. He dove down and grabbed him in his talons and flew up into the air. A great battle ensued as the KELŁOLEMEĆEN and the Thunderbird fought each other. The Thunderbird would drop the KELŁOLEMEĆEN and when he hit the water this would cause thunder and lightning. This is why we have thunder and lightning.

13 Killer Whale

Returning to The Picnic...

After we spot the KELȽOLEMEĆEN my sister and I get so excited that we forget those stupid rules

And we're like

YEAH! WOO! WOO!!

YEAH!!

And then

SIT DOWN!

HOLD HANDS!!

And then after a very long time

We finally make it to the shore of one of the W̱SÁNEĆ islands

ȽIW (Three) SX̱I,ÁM!!
Everyone together - ȽIW (Three) SX̱I,ÁM (Story)

One day, XÁLS gathered the W̱SÁNEĆ people from the village site called SṈIDȻEȽ. XÁLS picked up three black pebbles and threw them out over the water, and where they landed, three large mountains grew. One of those mountains was our sacred ȽÁU, WELṈEW̱ and another was PKOLS (the colonizers named it Mount Doug). XÁLS went to the top of the mountain and the W̱SÁNEĆ Peoples followed him. He then took some of the W̱SÁNEĆ People and tossed them into the waters where they changed into islands. XÁLS instructed the W̱SÁNEĆ Peoples to take care of their island relatives and for the island relatives to take care of the W̱SÁNEĆ Peoples. Therefore, those islands are collectively referred to as TETÁCES—Relatives of the deep.

Returning to The Picnic...

Our dad lifts us off the rowboat, one at a time

First me, and then my sister

Because we don't have a job, we take off right away

And we make a b-line right for our favorite spot

It's our mountain

Today we've decided we're going to conquer this mountain

So I start my sister off by helping her up

Get her started because she's only four and I'm five

And that's what we do, we help each other out together

So we make our way up the mountain

I'm climbing my way, I go past my sister

Getting closer and closer to the top

And all of a sudden somebody says

HEY, YOU KIDS!

GET DOWN FROM THERE!

But then we hear my dad say

Aww, leave 'em alone

They're fine

So we continue

Us getting closer to the top

And I get one hand over

Reach myself up

And the first thing I do?

I help my little sister up

Because I'm the big brother

She's four, and I'm five

And that's what we do when we're together

And the picture!

SNAP!

That picture

That picture was probably taken from

Probably right around here

CLICK!

My mom passed away suddenly

And at the funeral

My sister stood right there

Put her head on my shoulder, and cried

It was like she was four and I was five

And we were just trying to get through this together

And after the funeral we went through my mom's stuff

We came across a bunch of boxes

Photo albums

And we started looking through them

And there it was

That picture

Pshhh

And in the foreground, you can see my mom and dad

Sitting around the fire

And if you look off to the back you can see two little figures climbing up this small hill

I'm at the top and my sister is about three-quarters of the way up

She was four, I was five

And that's the day we conquered our mountain together

REFERENCES

Abbott, Larry. "Spiderwoman Theatre and the Tapestry of Story." *Canadian Journal of Native Studies* XVI, 1 (1996): 165–180.

Absolon, Kathleen E. (Minogiizhigokwe). *Kaandossiwin: How We Come to Know*. Halifax: Fernwood Publishing, 2011.

Alatas, Syed Farid. "Academic Dependency and the Global Division of Labour in the Social Sciences." *Current Sociology* 51, 6 (November, 2003): 599-613.

Alatas, Syed Farid. "The Sacralization of the Social Sciences: a Critique of an Emerging Theme in Academic Discourse." Archives de Sciences Sociales des Religions 40, 91 (July-Sept 1995): 89-111.

Alatas, Syed Hussein. "The Captive Mind and Creative Development," *International Social Science Journal* 26, 4 (1974): 691-700.

Alatas, Syed Hussein. "The Captive mind in development studies: Some neglected problems and the need for an autonomous social science tradition in Asia." *International Social Science Journal* XXIV, 1 (1972): 9–25.

Alfred, Gerald R.. *Peace, Power, Righteousness: An Indigenous Manifesto*. New York: Oxford University Press, 2009.

Alfred, Taiaiake. *Wasáse: Indigenous Pathways of Action and Freedom*. Toronto: University of Toronto Press, 2005.

Allen, Chadwick. "Blood (and) Memory." *American Literature* 71, 1 (1999): 93–116.

Amoss, Pamela. *Coast Salish Spirit Dancing: The Survival of an Ancestral Religion*. Seattle: University of Washington Press, 1978.

Amoss, Pamela. "The Power of Secrecy among the Coast Salish." In *The Anthropology of Power: Ethnographic Studies from Asia, Oceania and the New World*. Richard Adams, Ed.. New York: Academic Press, 1977. 131-139.

Anderson, Kim. *A Recognition of Being: Reconstructing Native Womanhood*. Toronto: Sumach Press, 2000.

Appleford, Rob, Ed.. *Aboriginal Drama and Theatre*. Toronto: Playwrights Canada Press, 2005.

Archibald, Jo-ann. *Indigenous Storywork: Educating the Heart, Mind, Body, and Spirit*. Vancouver: UBC Press, 2008.

Battiste, Marie. "Enabling the Autumn Seed: Toward a Decolonized Approach to Aboriginal Knowledge, Language, and Education." *Canadian Journal of Native Education* 22, 1 (1998): 16–27.

Battiste, Marie. *Reclaiming Indigenous Voice and Vision*. Vancouver: UBC Press, 2000.

Battiste, Marie, Lynne Bell, & L.M. Findlay. Decolonizing Education in Canadian Universities: An Interdisciplinary, International, Indigenous Research Project. *Canadian Journal of Native Education* 26, 2 (2002): 82–95.

Battiste, Marie, & The Government of Canada. "Indigenous Knowledge and Pedagogy in First Nations Education: A Literature Review with Recommendations." Ottawa: Minister's National Working Group on Education, 2002.

Bidal, Devon. "Archaeologists have unearthed exciting secrets on Haida Gwaii." *Hakai Magazine*, December 9, 2021. Retrieved March 28, 2022 from https://hakaimagazine.com/news/haida-gwaiis-caves-have-been-hiding-a-huge-secret/.

Boas, Franz. *Tsimshian Texts*. Washington, DC: Government Printing Office, 1902.

Boas, Franz, ed.. *Folk-tales of Salishan and Sahaptin Tribes*. New York: G.E. Strechert & Co., 1917.

Boas, Franz. *Kwakiutl Culture as Reflected in Mythology*. New York: G.E. Stechert & Co., 1935.

Borrows, John. *Canada's Indigenous Constitution*. Toronto: University of Toronto Press, 2010.

Botha, Louis. "Mixing Methods as a Process Towards Indigenous Methodologies." *International Journal of Social Research Methodology* 14, 4 (2011): 313–325. doi:10.1080/13645579.2010.516644.

Brayboy, Byan and Emma Maughn. "Indigenous Knowledges and the Story of the Bean." *Harvard Educational Review* 79, 1 (April 2009): 1–21.

Brown, Leslie and Susan Strega, Eds.. *Research as Resistance: Critical, Indigenous, and Anti-Oppressive Approaches*. Toronto: Canadian Scholars' Press, 2005.

Cajete, Gregory. *Native Science: Natural Laws of Interdependence*. Santa Fe: Clear Light Publishers, 2000.

Canada, "Interagency Advisory Panel on Research Ethics." Retrieved August 26, 2022. https://ethics.gc.ca/eng/policy-politique_tcps2-eptc2_2018.html.

Canada. *Statement of the Government of Canada on Indian Policy, 1969*. [White Paper]. Prepared by Jean Chretién. Department of Indian Affairs and Northern Development. Ottawa: Queen's Printer, 1969.

Canada. *Tri-council Policy Statement: Ethical Conduct for Research Involving Humans* – TCPS 2, I. A. P. on R. E. (2020, February 19), 2018.

Claxton, Earle and John Elliott. *The Saanich Year*. Saanich Indian School Board, 1993. Booklet #63.

Claxton, Nicholas Xemtoltw. *The Douglas Treaty and WSÁNEC Traditional Fisheries: A Model for Saanich Peoples' Governance*. Unpublished MA thesis, University of Victoria, 2003. Retrieved from http://web.uvic.ca/igov/index.php/igov-598-community-governance-project.

Claxton, Nicholas Xemtoltw. *To Fish as Formerly: A Resurgent Journey back to the Saanich Reef Net Fishery*. Unpublished PhD dissertation, University of Victoria, 2015. Retrieved from http://hdl.handle.net/1828/6614.

Claxton, Nicholas Xemtoltw. "To Fish as Formerly": The Douglas Treaties and the W̱SÁNEĆ Reef-net Fisheries." In *Lighting the Eighth Fire: The Liberation, Resurgence, and Protection of Indigenous Nations*. Winnipeg: ARP Books, 2008. 47–58.

Corntassel, Jeff J.. "An activist posing as an academic?" *American Indian Quarterly* 27, 1/2 (2004): 160-171.

Cote-Meek, Sheila. *Colonized Classrooms: Racism, Trauma and Resistance in Post-Secondary Education*. Winnipeg / Halifax: Fernwood Publishing, 2014.

Cruikshank, Julie. *Do Glaciers listen? Local Knowledge, Colonial Encounters, & Social Imagination*. Vancouver: UBC Press, 2005.

Cruikshank, Julie. *Life Lived like a Story: Life Stories of Three Native Yukon Elders*. Vancouver: UBC Press, 1990.

Dei, George J. Sefa, Dorothy Goldin Rosenberg, and Budd L. Hall. *Indigenous Knowledges in Global Contexts: Multiple Readings of Our Worlds*. Toronto: University of Toronto Press, 2002.

Deloria, Vine. *God is Ted: A Native View of Religion*. Golden, CO: North American Press, 1994.

Denzin, Norman K., and Yvonna S. Lincoln. *The SAGE Handbook of Qualitative Research*. Thousand Oaks: Sage Publications, 2005.

Doerfler, Jill, Niigaanwewidam James Sinclair, and Heidi Kiiwetinepinesiik Stark. *Centering Anishinaabeg Studies: Understanding the World through Stories*. East Lansing, MI: Michigan State University Press, 2013.

Drawson, Alexandra S., Elaine Toombs. and Christopher J. Mushquash, "Indigenous Research Methods: A Systematic Review." *The International Indigenous Policy Journal* 8, 2 (2017): 1–25. DOI: 10.18584/iipj.2017.8.2.5.

Duff, Wilson. "The Fort Victoria Treaties." *Journal of BC Studies* 3 (fall 1969): 3–57.

Duff, Wilson. *The Upper Stolo Indians of the Fraser Valley, British Columbia*. Victoria: British Columbia Provincial Museum, Dept. of Education, 1952.

Edmonds, Penelope. "Unpacking Settler Colonialism's Urban Strategies: Indigenous Peoples in Victoria, British Columbia, and the Transition to a Settler-Colonial City." *Urban History Review/ Revue D'Histoire Urbaine* 38, 2 (2010): 4–20.

Elliot Sr., Dave *Saltwater People: As Told by Dave Elliot Sr.*. Saanich School District, 1983. #63.

Ellis, Carolyn, Tony E. Adams, and Arthur P. Bochner. Autoethnography: An Overview [40 paragraphs]. *Forum Qualitative Sozialforschung / Forum: Qualitative Social Research* 12, 1 (2011). https://doi.org/10.17169/fqs-12.1.1589.

Episkenew, Jo-Ann. *Taking Back Our Spirits: Indigenous Literature, Public Policy, and Healing*. Winnipeg: University of Manitoba Press, 2009.

Ermine, Willie. "Aboriginal Epistemology." In *First Nations Education in Canada: The Circle Unfolds,* Marie Battiste and Jean Barman Eds.. Vancouver: UBC Press, 1995. 101–112.

Fals-Borda, Orlando, and Md Anisur Rahman, *Action and Knowledge: Breaking the Monopoly With Participatory Action-Research.* New York / London: Apex Press, 1991.

Fixico, Donald L.. *The American Indian Mind in a Linear World: American Indian studies and Traditional Knowledge.* New York: Routledge, 2003.

Freire, Paulo. *Pedagogy of the Oppressed.* New York: Continuum, 2000.

Gaudry, Adam. "Insurgent Research." *Wicazo Sa Review* 26, 1 (2011): 113–136.

Goffman, Erving. *The Presentation of Self in Everyday Life.* New York: Anchor Books, 1959.

Graveline, Fyre Jean. *Circleworks: Transforming Eurocentric Consciousness.* Halifax, Fernwood Publishing, 1998.

Guba, Egon G. and Yvonna S. Lincoln. "Competing Paradigms in Qualitative Research." *Handbook of Qualitative Research*, Norman K. Denzin & Yvonna S. Lincoln, Eds.. Thousand Oaks: Sage Publishing. 1994. 105-117.

Hamlisch, Kirkwood J., Dante, N., Kleban, E., & Noeltner, R. H. (1977). *A chorus line*. Edwin H. Morris & Company, 1977. (No location).

Harris, Cole. "How Did Dolonialism Dispossess? Comments from the Edge of Empire," *Annals of the Association of American Geographers*, 94, 1 (2004): 165–182.

Harris, Cole. *Making Native Space: Colonialism, Resistance, and Reserves in British Columbia.* Vancouver: UBC Press, 2002.

Harris, Cole. *The Resettlement of British Columbia: Essays on Colonialism and Geographical Change.* Vancouver: UBC Press, 1997.

Harris, Douglas C.. "A Court Between: Aboriginal and Treaty Rights in the British Columbia Court of Appeal." *BC Studies* 162 (2009): 137–164.

Harris, Douglas C.. *Landing Native Fisheries: Indian Reserves and Fishing Rights in British Columbia, 1849–1925*. Vancouver: UBC Press, 2008.

Hauknes, John, and Mark Knell. "Embodied Knowledge and Sectoral Linkages: Input–output Approach to the Interaction of High- and Low-tech Industries," *Research Policy* 38, 3 (2009). 459–469.

Heron, John, and Peter Reason. "A Participatory Inquiry Paradigm." *Qualitative Inquiry* 3, 3 (1997): 274-294.

Heth, Charlotte., and National Museum of the American Indian (U.S.). "Native American dance: Ceremonies and social traditions." National Museum of the American Indian, Smithsonian Institution, with Starwood Pub., 1992.

Highway Thompson. *Dry Lips Oughta Move to Kapuskasing : A Play*. Saskatoon: Fifth House, 1989.

Horne, Jack. *The Picnic*. YouTube recording, 2015. Retrieved October 14, 2021, from https://studio.youtube.com/video/z9CSjqP_84U/edit.

Horne, Jack. "W̱SÁNEĆ: Emerging Land or Emerging People." *The Arbutus Review* 3, 2 (2012) 6–19.

Indian Association of Alberta. *Citizens Plus* [Red Paper]. Prepared by Harold Cardinal. 1970. https://www.thecanadianencyclopedia.ca/en/article/citizens-plus-the-red-paper

Jacobs, Don Trent (Four Arrows). *The Authentic Dissertation: Alternative Ways of Knowing, Research, and Representation.* London & New York: Taylor & Francis, 2008.

Kidd, Ross. "Reclaiming Culture: Indigenous Performers Take Back Their Show." *The Canadian Journal Of Native Studies* 4, 1 (1984): 105-120.

King, Thomas. *The Truth About Stories: A Native Narrative*. Toronto: House of Anansi Press, 2003.

Kirkness, Verna J. & Barnhardt, Ray "First Nations and Higher Education: The Four R's—Respect, Relevance, Reciprocity, Responsibility." *Journal of American Indian Education* 30, 3 (1991): 1–15.

Knowles, Richard Paul, and Monique Mojica, Eds.. "Introduction." In *Staging Coyote's Dream: An Anthology of First Nations Drama in English,* Toronto: Playwrights Canada Press, 2003. iii-vii.

Korb, Scott, and Lewis H. Lapham. "Useful Ignorance." Lapham's Quarterly, January 1, 1970. https://www.laphamsquarterly.org/ways-learning/useful-ignorance.

Kovach, Margaret. "Conversational Method in Indigenous Research." *First Peoples Child and Family Review* 5,1 (2010) 40–48.

Kovach, Margaret. *Indigenous Methodologies: Characteristics, Conversations, and Contexts*. Toronto: University of Toronto Press, 2009.

Laduke, Winona. *All our Relations: Native Struggles for Land and Life*. Cambridge MA: South End Press / Honor the Earth, 1999.

Lambright, Anne. "A Nation Embodied: Woman in the Work of Yuyachkani." *Letras Femeninas*, 35, 2 (winter 2009): 133–152.

Lara, Anna-Maurine. "The Spirit of the Ancestors: The Photography and Installation Art of Albert Chong and Wura-Natasha Ogunji." *Canadian Woman Studies* 23, 2 (2004): 14–20.

Lincoln, Yvonna S., and Egon G. Guba. "Paradigmatic Controversies, Contradictions, and Emerging Confluences." In *The SAGE Handbook of Qualitative Research*, Norman K. Denzin, Yvonna S. Lincoln Eds.. Thousand Oaks: Sage Publications, 2005.

Little Bear, Leroy. "Jagged Worldviews Colliding." In *Reclaiming Indigenous Voices and Vision,* Marie Battiste, Ed.. Vancouver: UBC Press, 2000. 77–85.

Madhavan, Ravindranath, and Rajiv Grover. "From Embedded Knowledge to Embodied Knowledge: New Product Development as Knowledge Management." *Journal of Marketing* 6, 4 (1998). 1–12.

Madison, D. Soyini. *Acts of Activism: Human Rights as Radical Performance* (*Theatre and Performance Theory*). Cambridge: Cambridge University Press, 2010.

Malewski, Erik, and Nathalia Jaramillo, Eds.. *Epistemologies of Ignorance in Education*. Charlotte, NC: Information Age Publishing, 2011.

Mankiewicz, Francis., Dir. *Conspiracy of Silence*. Written by Suzette Couture & Lisa Priest. Canadian Broadcasting Corporation, aired Dec 1 & 2, 1991. Astral Video. 1993.

Maracle, Lee. *I am Woman: A Native Perspective on Sociology and Feminism*. Vancouver: Press Gang Publishers, 1996.

McKee, Christopher. *Treaty Talks in British Columbia: Negotiating a Mutually Beneficial Future*. Vancouver: UBC Press, 1996.

McKee, Christopher. *Treaty Talks in British Columbia: Building a New Relationship*. Vancouver: UBC Press, 2009.

McLeod, Neal. *Cree Narrative Memory: From Treaties to Dontemporary Times*. Saskatoon: Purich Publishing, 2007.

Memmi, Albert. *The Colonizer and the Colonized*. Howard Greenfeld, Trans. London: Orion Press, 1965.

Menzies, Heather. "From Knowing Bodies to Global Knowledge Systems." *Topia: Canadian Journal of Cultural Studies* 15 (Spring 2006): 103–108.

Metcalfe, Tom. "Fossil footprints show humans in North America more than 21,000 years ago," NBCNews.com, September 23, 2021.

Retrieved March 28, 2022, from https://www.nbcnews.com/science/science-news/fossil-footprints-show-humans-north-america-21000-years-ago-rcna2169.

Meyer, Manulani Aluli. *Hawaiian Knowing: Old Ways for Feeing a New World*. Hawaii: Koa Books, 1998.

Mignolo, Walter D.. "Epistemic Disobedience, Independent Thought and De-colonial Freedom." *Theory, Culture & Society* 26 (2009): 159–181.

Mignolo, Walter D. "Spirit Out of Bounds Returns to the East: The Closing of the Social Sciences and the Opening of Independent Thoughts." *Current Sociology* 62, 4 (2014): 584–602.

Mihesuah, Devon A. *Natives and Academics: Researching and Writing About American Indians*. Lincoln, NE: University of Nebraska Press, 1998.

Mills, Antonia Curtze. *Eagle down is Our Law: Witsuwit'en Law, Feasts, and Land Claims*. Vancouver: UBC Press, 1994.

Mojica, Monique. "Stories From the Body: Blood Memory and Organic Texts." In *Native American Performance and Representation*, S. E. Wilmer, Ed.. Tucson: University of Arizona Press, 2009. 97–109.

Mojica, Monique, and Rick Knowles. *Staging Coyote's Dream: An Anthology of First Nations Drama in English*. Toronto: Playwrights Canada Press, 2009.

Momaday, N. Scott. *House Made of Dawn*. New York: New American Library, 1969.

Monture-Angus, Patricia. *Thunder in My Soul: A Mohawk Woman Speaks*. Halifax: Fernwood Publishing, 1995.

Murphy, Jacqueline Shea. *The People Have Never Stopped Dancing: Native American Modern Dance Histories*. Minneapolis: University of Minnesota Press, 2007.

Murton, James. *Creating a Modern Countryside: Liberalism and Land Resettlement in British Columbia*. Vancouver: UBC Press, 2009.

Ngũgĩ, wa Thiong'o, *Decolonizing the Mind: The Politics of Language in African Literature*. London; Nairobi; Portsmouth, NH: J. Currey, 1986.

Office of Strategic Services. *Simple Sabotage Field Manual: Strategic Services (Provisional)*. Washington, D.C., 1944. Retrieved from: https://www.gutenberg.org/files/26184/page-images/26184-images.pdf.

Rabinow, Paul, Ed.. *The Foucault Reader*. London: Puffin, 1991.

Regan, Paulette. *Unsettling the Settler Within: Indian Residential Schools, Truth Telling, and Reconciliation in Canada*. Vancouver: UBC Press, 2010.

Sage, Walter N., "The Oregon Treaty of 1846." *Canadian Historical Review* 27,1 (1946).

Santos, Boaventura de Sousa. *The End of the Cognitive Empire: the Coming of Age of Epistemologies of the South*. Durham: Duke University Press, 2018.

Schechner, Richard. *The Future of Ritual: Writings on Culture and Performance*. Abingdon, Oxfordshire: Routledge, 1993.

Schechner, Richard. *Performance Theory*. New York: Routledge, 1988.

Schechner, Richard, and Victor Turner, *Between Theater & Anthropology*. Philadelphia: University of Pennsylvania Press, 1985.

Schenke, Arleen, and Handel Wright. "Baffling Power: History, Pedagogy and Body Politics—An Interview with Philip Corrigan." *Left History: An Interdisciplinary Journal of Historical Inquiry and Debate* 3, 2 (1996): 249–264.

Shore, Randy. "Heiltsuk First Nation Village among oldest in North America: Archeologists." *Vancouver Sun* March 29, 2017. Retrieved March 28, 2022, from https://vancouversun.com/news/local-news/heiltsuk-first-nation-village-among-oldest-in-north-america-archeologists.

Shorter, David Delgado. *We Will Dance our truth: Yaqui History in Yoeme Performance*. Lincoln, NB: University of Nebraska Press, 2009.

Simpson, Leanne Betasamosake. *As We Have Always Done: Indigenous Freedom Through Radical Resistance*. Minneapolis: University of Minnesota Press, 2017.

Simpson, Leanne Betasamosake. "Bubbling Like a Beating Heart": Reflections on Nishnaabeg Poetic and Narrative Consciousness." In *Indigenous Poetics in Canada*, Neal McLeod, Ed.. Waterloo, ON: Wilfred Laurier University Press, 2014. 107-120.

Simpson, Leanne Betasamosake. *Dancing on Our Turtle's Back: Stories of Nishnaabeg Re-creation, Resurgence and a New Emergence*. Winnipeg: ARP Books, 2011.

Simpson, Leanne Betasamosake. *The Gift is in the Making: Anishinaabeg Stories*. Winnipeg: HighWater Press, 2013.

Smith, Graham Hingangaroa. "Indigenous Struggle for the Transformation of Education and Schooling," The University of Auckland, Keynote Address to the Alaskan Federation of Natives (AFN) Convention, Anchorage, Alaska, 2003. Retrieved December 11, 2021 from: http://www.ankn.uaf.edu/curriculum/Articles/GrahamSmith/.

Smith, Linda Tuhiwai. *Decolonizing Methodologies: Research and Indigenous Peoples*. 2nd edition. London / New York: Zed Books, 2012.

Spiderwoman Theatre. *Muriel Miguel: A Retrospective*, 2015. Retrieved from http://www.spiderwomantheater.org/workshop.htm.

Spiderwoman Theater. *Spiderwoman Theater*, n.d.. Retrieved March 28, 2022, from https://www.spiderwomantheater.org/.

Spooner, Mark. "Eve Tuck: Biting the Hand That Feeds You." YouTube, 2015, August 12. Retrieved October 17, 2021, from https://www.youtube.com/watch?v=lXEEzqIjA3I.

Sunseri, Lina. *Being Again of One Mind: Oneida Women and the Struggle for Decolonization*. Vancouver: UBC Press, 2011.

Taylor, Diana. *The Archive and the Repertoire: Performing Cultural Memory in the Americas*. Durham: Duke University Press, 2003.

Trent University. "Trent University Indigenous Studies Ph.D. Program Student Handbook 2014–2015." 2014.

Tuck, Eve, and K. Wayne Yang. "Decolonization is Not a Metaphor." *Decolonization, Indigeneity, Education, & Society, Journal Publishing Services* 1, 1 (2012).

Turner, Dale. *This is Not a Peace Pipe: Towards a Critical Indigenous Philosophy*. Toronto: University of Toronto Press, 2006.

Turner, Victor. *The Anthropology of Performance*. New York: PAJ Publications, 1986.

Turner, Victor. *From Ritual to Theatre: The Human Seriousness of Play*. New York: PAJ Publications. 1982.

Universities Canada. "Universities Canada principles on Indigenous education." 2015. Retrieved from: https://www.univcan.ca/media-room/media-releases/universities-canada-principles-on-indigenous-education/.

Wallerstein, Immanuel. "Open the Social Sciences." *Items: Social Science Research Council* 50, 1 (1996): 1-6.

Warrior, Robert Allen. *The People and the Word: Reading Native Nonfiction*. Minneapolis: University of Minnesota Press, 2005.

Weaver, Jace. *That the People Might Live: Native American Literatures and Native American Community*. New York: Oxford University Press, 1997.

Weber-Pillwax, Cora. "What is Indigenous Research?" *Canadian Journal of Native Education* 25, 2 (2001): 166–174.

Wheeler, Winona. "Reflections on the Social Relations of Indigenous Oral Histories." In *Walking a Tightrope: Aboriginal People and Their Representations,* David T. McNab Ed., Waterloo: Wilfrid Laurier University Press, 2005. 189-214.

Wilson, Shawn. *Research is Ceremony: Indigenous Research Methods*. Blackpoint, NS: Fernwood

Publishing, 2008.

Wolf-Michael R., & A.C. Barton. *Rethinking Scientific Literature*. New York: Routledge Falmer, 2004.

Woolford, Andrew. *Between Justice and Certainty: The British Columbia Treaty Process*. UBC Press, 2005.

W̱SÁNEĆ community members, Saanich Adult Education Centre, Saanich Indian School Board. *ÁLENENEC: Learning from Homeland*. Saanich Indian School Board, 2008.

Jack Horne is a proud member of the W̱SÁNEĆ Nation on Vancouver Island. His mom Elsie Smith is from the WJOLEP community, and his dad George Horne is from the TSAWOUṮ community. WJOLEP and TSAWOUT are two of four reserve communities that make up the W̱SÁNEĆ Nation. Jack's first career was in the performing arts, and when he retired from theatre he returned to post-secondary education. He received a BA from the University of Victoria, an MA from York University, and he completed a PhD in Indigenous Studies from Trent University. Jack's focus during his education journey has unwaveringly been on Indigenous, and specifically W̱SÁNEĆ perspectives.

HÍSW̱ḴE SIAM